YVONNE VERA was born and brought up in Bulawayo, Zimbabwe. She studied at and gained her Ph.D. from York University in Canada. She now works as the Director of the National Gallery of Zimbabwe in Bulawayo. Yvonne Vera is the author of the novels *Nehanda* (1993), *Without a Name* (1994), *Under the Tongue* (1996), and *Butterfly Burning* (1998), as well as the short-story collection *Why Don't You Carve Other Animals* (1992), all published by Baobab Books. (*Why Don't You Carve Other Animals* was first published by TSAR Publications, Toronto.) *Without a Name* and *Under the Tongue* both won first prize in the Zimbabwe Publishers' Literary Awards of 1995 and 1997 respectively. *Under the Tongue* won the 1997 Commonwealth Writers Prize (Africa Region). Yvonne Vera won the Swedish literary award The Voice of Africa 1999.

OPENING SPACES

An Anthology of Contemporary African Women's Writing

Edited by
YVONNE VERA

Heinemann

BAOBAB BOOKS

To Sasa, Koye and Khethi with embraces

Heinemann Educational Publishers
Halley Court, Jordan Hill, Oxford OX2 8EJ
A Division of Reed Educational & Professional Publishing Limited

Heinemann: A Division of Reed Publishing (USA) Inc.
361 Hanover Street, Portsmouth, NH 03801–3912, USA

Heinemann Publishers (Pty) Limited
PO Box 781940, Sandton 2146, Johannesburg, South Africa

OXFORD   MELBOURNE   AUCKLAND
JOHANNESBURG   BLANTYRE   GABORONE
IBADAN   PORTSMOUTH (NH) USA   CHICAGO

Baobab Books
Box 567, Harare, Zimbabwe

First published by Heinemann Educational Publishers/
Baobab Books in 1999

British Library Cataloguing in Publication Data
A catalogue record for this book is available from the British Library.

Cover design by Touchpaper
The publisher would like to acknowledge the help of the
National Gallery of Zimbabwe in producing the cover.

Printed and bound in Great Britain by
Cox and Wyman Ltd, Reading, Berkshire

ISBN 0 435 91010 8

99 00 01 02 7 6 5 4 3 2 1

CONTENTS

PL
8011
064
1989

v

CONTENTS

Preface

A woman writer must have an imagination that is plain stubborn, that can invent new gods and banish ineffectual ones.

I remember a scene from the film *Sankofa* in which a pregnant woman is whipped to death on a slave plantation. The rest of the women, about a dozen, buzz forward like locusts. They are embraced in enigmatic yet shattering voices. Then these women with hope calcified, with a desire to rescue and set free, circle the deceased and protect her with their bodies. Their gesture is a bold risk. So they stand close in seething intimacy in that dank land with no sky which they can claim, they raise sugar-cane cutters into the air and keep them there in a frantic salute to their predicament, their arms like hewn branches. In this, they offer a slim privacy to the corpse as it gives birth; its motions captured by the camera as the head now lying on the ground swings from side to side, side to side, in eloquent silence. These women remind us, poignantly, what a woman is, what a man is not. Here, birth becomes an aberration that comments on the ruthless circumstance of a female agony occurring in a stultifying, thoroughly confusing construct of authority. Whatever the woman meant to speak has not died in her mouth. Instead we discover the stunning ability of the silenced to triumph over adversity. Within this incredible circle of raised arms dripping with the sweet juice of sugar cane and forced labour, the women weep a combined eulogy that allows the child to emerge, at once commodity, at once human. The mother dead, the enslaved women woven into the tightest despair. Throughout this scene, the film screen becomes too static, too brief for this climax of ritual. The viewer is transposed into the trembling tones of these women's voices so strong and rich, so uniquely knowing. Nothing is obvious any more except that double oppression. The *griot*[1] among them, carrying the spirit of Africa intact in her mouth, calls to all the histories of a woman's world. She brims with tears, a maddening mimicry and song – clutching at her own sanity like a dead root. As in writing, sometimes a single moment in cinema speaks across several genres: the visual, the oral, the tragic.

Hopefully this short-story collection proves that women from Africa have not been swallowed by history, that they too know how to swallow history. Their writing may best reveal how desperately Africa has erred in its memory. The women, without power to govern, often have no platform for expressing their disapproval, even their *mihloti*, the tears Mirian Tlali once described so intensely. Like pods, some of these women merely explode. Words become weapons.

Africa is as diverse in its womanhood as it is in its disillusionment. Our reference to an African womanhood is a mere trope, a way of ordering, much too limiting. Yet the purpose of an anthology is also to create unities, to motivate strengths, and offer a signature. Such an aim is noble and complete. There are many possibilities for selection. In this collection the aim is to create a circle as real as the women protecting that seemingly impossible birth above – joined by land, by the evidence of the eyes, by current struggles, by a hunger for escape. We ought to write bravely, fiercely. Tsitsi Dangarembga opens her novel *Nervous Conditions* with the following, 'I was not sorry when my brother died.' This is a shocking statement which I cannot

[1] Community spokesperson with spiritual authority.

imagine uttered in a room full of uncles, grandmothers, parents or siblings. Moreover, being uttered by a woman, without preamble; the head bowed for example, the knees bending, the voice disguised and apologetic, the voice bending even further than the knees ever can reach. None of this. In the culture in which Dangarembga's pronouncement is set, such a statement would make clear that the speaker has been abandoned by her ancestors and all acts of healing summoned.

Dangarembga does not apologize for the taboo in her mouth. For being a witness. If speaking is still difficult to negotiate, then writing has created a free space for most women – much freer than speech. There is less interruption, less immediate and shocked reaction. The written text is granted its intimacy, its privacy, its creation of a world, its proposals, its individual characters, its suspension of disbelief. It surprises in the best carnival way, reducing distances, accepting the least official stance. The book is bound, circulated, read. It retains its autonomy much more than a woman is allowed in the oral situation. Writing offers a moment of intervention.

I know the intense risk a woman takes in the sheer effort of writing, placing herself beyond the accepted margin, abandoning the securities of less daunting, much more approved paths. It is an act of courage that she writes and releases those vital secrets. She participates in that shaking birth occurring in the midst of stunned wonder. She is the dreamer and storyteller, the one Bessie Head envisaged with so much idealism – the broken shards come together, and the thunder behind her ears subsides.

This collection celebrates recent writing from women in Africa. No longer writing to empire as our early writers did, a variety of themes and preoccupations emerge, each engaged through the prism of a combined womanhood. 'Night Thoughts' by Monde Sifuniso is a meditation. As in Ama Ata Aidoo's tantalizing ironies in 'The Girl Who Can', this story is rich with satiric observation. Where Aidoo criticizes the politics surrounding the female body in cultural practice, Sifuniso challenges political authority in Africa and its often absurd indecency. The technical facility and writing skill of Sifuniso and Aidoo find companionship in the cryptic, intense sophistication of Mauritian writer Lindsey Collen's 'The Enigma'. A brief tale where, right from its opening, discordant tonalities leap off the page. The tensions of relationships between the genders are explored.

Sudan's Leila Aboulela welcomes the reader of 'The Museum' with a controlled and confident exploration of a woman in exile as she ponders the dichotomies of arranged marriages, the transforming power of an overseas education, the imbalance of family ties, the nature of love. Aboulela's language is firm as she guides the reader through each phrase, each pause and illumination. Like Aidoo, Sifuniso and Collen, she too basks in ironies and reversals.

Véronique Tadjo's 'The Betrayal' is memorable in the kind of world it creates. As the story unfolds, the range of possible experiences suggested increasingly surpasses the ordinary world of daily contact.

There is a brave searching voice in Gugu Ndlovu's 'The Barrel of a Pen'. Set in a sordid hotel, familiar details become visible and jarring; a bell, a torn curtain, a knock on the door. Meanwhile, Chiedza Musengezi's 'Crocodile Tails' reveals cultural clashes as an expatriate community emerges in a recently independent state. Questions of female identity and intimacy become vital and threatening.

Ifeoma Okoye's 'The Power of a Plate of Rice' illustrates the routine oppression of many African women, and the indomitable spirit which rises up to face this oppression.

'Stress' carefully delineates a woman's unfortunate disintegration and corruption. Lília Momplé allows the story to develop slowly, moment by moment, tracing the mood of the major-general's lover. It is a choreographed piece in which the decadent and dangerous somnambulism of this main character is as cloying as it is fascinating.

In 'The Red Velvet Dress' Farida Karodia explores the difficulty of domestic relationships; the effort at forgiveness, the triumph of truth, the beauty of belonging. Sindiwe Magona's 'A State of Outrage' and Norma Kitson's 'Uncle Bunty' similarly confirm the exciting courage of a post-apartheid creative effort. In 'A Perfect Wife', 'The Home-Coming' and 'Deciduous Gazettes' the authors Anna Dao, Milly Jafta and Melissa Tandiwe Myambo each offer yet other prisms, other means of exploring the passage of time, and the kinship which survives among women in the midst of betrayals and absences.

Together, the women in this anthology prove that the woman writer in Africa is a witness; forgiving the evidence of the eyes, pronouncing her experience with insight, artistry, and a fertile dexterity. Her response to theme, event, taboo is vital and pressing.

Here, our witnesses, in that seemingly impossible birth.

Yvonne Vera, 1999

AMA ATA AIDOO

The Girl Who Can

They say that I was born in Hasodzi; and it is a very big village in the central region of our country, Ghana. They also say that when all of Africa is not choking under a drought, Hasodzi lies in a very fertile lowland in a district known for its good soil. Maybe that is why any time I don't finish eating my food, Nana says, 'You Adjoa, you don't know what life is about . . . you don't know what problems there are in this life . . .'

As far as I could see, there was only one problem. And it had nothing to do with what I knew Nana considered as 'problems', or what Maami thinks of as 'the problem'. Maami is my mother. Nana is my mother's mother. And they say I am seven years old. And my problem is that at this seven years of age, there are things I can think in my head, but which, maybe, I do not have the proper language to speak them out with. And that, I think, is a very serious problem because it is always difficult to decide whether to keep quiet and not say any of the things that come into my head, or say them and get laughed at. Not that it is easy to get any grown-up to listen to you, even when you decide to take the risk and say something serious to them.

Take Nana. First, I have to struggle to catch her attention. Then I tell her something I had taken a long time to figure out. And then you know what always happens? She would at once stop whatever she is doing and, mouth open, stare at me for a very long time. Then, bending and turning her head slightly, so that one ear comes down towards me, she'll say in *that* voice: 'Adjoa, you say what?' After I have repeated whatever I had said, she would either, still in that voice, ask me 'never, never, but NEVER to repeat THAT', or she would immediately burst out laughing. She would laugh and laugh and laugh, until tears run down her cheeks and she would stop whatever she is doing and wipe away the tears with the hanging edges of her cloth. And she would continue laughing until she is completely tired. But then, as soon as another person comes by, just to make sure she doesn't forget whatever it was I had said, she would repeat it to her. And then, of course, there would be two old people laughing and screaming with tears running down their faces. Sometimes this show continues until there are three, four or even more of such laughing and screaming tear-faced grown-ups. And all that performance for whatever I'd said? I find something quite confusing in all this. That is, no one ever explains to me why sometimes I shouldn't repeat some things I say; while at other times, some other things I say would not only be all right, but would be considered so funny they would be repeated so many times for so many people's enjoyment. You see how neither way of hearing me out can encourage me to express my thoughts too often?

Like all this business to do with my legs. I have always wanted to tell them not to worry. I mean Nana and my mother. It did not have to be an issue for my two favourite people to fight over. I didn't want to be told not to repeat it or for it to be considered so funny that anyone would laugh at me until they cried. After all, they were my legs . . . When I think back on it now, those two, Nana and my mother must have been discussing my legs from the day I was born. What I am sure of is that when I came out of the land of sweet, soft silence into the world of noise and comprehension, the first topic I met was my legs.

That discussion was repeated very regularly.

Nana: 'Ah, ah, you know, Kaya, I thank my God that your

very first child is female. But Kaya, I am not sure about her legs. Hm . . . hm . . . hm . . .'

And Nana would shake her head.

Maami: 'Mother, why are you always complaining about Adjoa's legs? If you ask me . . .'

Nana: 'They are too thin. And I am not asking you!'

Nana has many voices. There is a special one she uses to shut everyone up.

'Some people have no legs at all,' my mother would try again with all her small courage.

'But Adjoa has legs,' Nana would insist; 'except that they are too thin. And also too long for a woman. Kaya, listen. Once in a while, but only once in a very long while, somebody decides – nature, a child's spirit mother, an accident happens, and somebody gets born without arms, or legs, or both sets of limbs. And then let me touch wood; it is a sad business. And you know, such things are not for talking about everyday. But if any female child decides to come into this world with legs, then they might as well be legs.'

'What kind of legs?' And always at that point, I knew from her voice that my mother was weeping inside. Nana never heard such inside weeping. Not that it would have stopped Nana even if she had heard it. Which always surprised me. Because, about almost everything else apart from my legs, Nana is such a good grown-up. In any case, what do I know about good grown-ups and bad grown-ups? How could Nana be a good grown-up when she carried on so about my legs? All I want to say is that I really liked Nana except for that.

Nana: 'As I keep saying, if any woman decides to come into this world with her two legs, then she should select legs that have meat on them: with good calves. Because you are sure such legs would support solid hips. And a woman must have solid hips to be able to have children.'

9

'Oh, Mother.' That's how my mother would answer. Very, very quietly. And the discussion would end or they would move on to something else.

Sometimes, Nana would pull in something about my father:

How, 'Looking at such a man, we have to be humble and admit that after all, God's children are many . . .'

How, 'After one's only daughter had insisted on marrying a man like that, you still have to thank your God that the biggest problem you got later was having a granddaughter with spindly legs that are too long for a woman, and too thin to be of any use.'

The way she always added that bit about my father under her breath, she probably thought I didn't hear it. But I always heard it. Plus, that is what always shut my mother up for good, so that even if I had not actually heard the words, once my mother looked like even her little courage was finished, I could always guess what Nana had added to the argument.

'Legs that have meat on them with good calves to support solid hips . . . to be able to have children.'

So I wished that one day I would see, for myself, the legs of any woman who had had children. But in our village, that is not easy. The older women wear long wrap-arounds all the time. Perhaps if they let me go bathe in the river in the evening, I could have checked. But I never had the chance. It took a lot of begging just to get my mother and Nana to let me go splash around in the shallow end of the river with my friends, who were other little girls like me. For proper baths, we used the small bathhouse behind our hut. Therefore, the only naked female legs I have ever really seen are those of other little girls like me, or older girls in the school. And those of my mother and Nana: two pairs of legs which must surely belong to the approved kind; because Nana gave birth to my mother and my mother gave birth to me. In my eyes, all my friends have got legs that look like legs, but whether the legs have got meat on them to support the kind of hips that . . . that I don't know.

◆

According to the older boys and girls, the distance between our little village and the small town is about five kilometres. I don't know what five kilometres mean. They always complain about how long it is to walk to school and back. But to me, we live in our village, and walking those kilometres didn't matter. School is nice.

School is another thing Nana and my mother discussed often and appeared to have different ideas about. Nana thought it would be a waste of time. I never understood what she meant. My mother seemed to know – and disagreed. She kept telling Nana that she – that is, my mother – felt she was locked into some kind of darkness because she didn't go to school. So that if I, her daughter, could learn to write and read my own name and a little besides – perhaps be able to calculate some things on paper – that would be good. I could always marry later and maybe . . .

Nana would just laugh. 'Ah, maybe with legs like hers, she might as well go to school.'

Running with our classmates on our small sports field and winning first place each time never seemed to me to be anything about which to tell anyone at home. This time it was different. I don't know how the teachers decided to let me run for the junior section of our school in the district games. But they did.

When I went home to tell my mother and Nana, they had not believed it at first. So Nana had taken it upon herself to go and 'ask into it properly'. She came home to tell my mother that it was really true. I was one of my school's runners.

'Is that so?' exclaimed my mother. I know her. Her mouth

moved as though she was going to tell Nana, that, after all, there was a secret about me she couldn't be expected to share with anyone. But then Nana herself looked so pleased, out of surprise, my mother shut her mouth up. In any case, since the first time they heard the news, I have often caught Nana staring at my legs with a strange look on her face, but still pretending like she was not looking. All this week, she has been washing my school uniform herself. That is a big surprise. And she didn't stop at that, she even went to Mr Mensah's house and borrowed his charcoal pressing iron. Each time she came back home with it and ironed and ironed and ironed the uniform, until, if I had been the uniform, I would have said aloud that I had had enough.

Wearing my school uniform this week has been very nice. At the parade, on the first afternoon, its sheen caught the rays of the sun and shone brighter than anybody else's uniform. I'm sure Nana saw that too, and must have liked it. Yes, she has been coming into town with us every afternoon of this district sports week. Each afternoon, she has pulled one set of fresh old cloth from the big brass bowl to wear. And those old clothes are always so stiffly starched, you can hear the cloth creak when she passes by. But she walks way behind us schoolchildren. As though she was on her own way to some place else.

Yes, I have won every race I ran for my school, and I have won the cup for the best all-round junior athlete. Yes, Nana said that she didn't care if such things are not done. She would do it. You know what she did? She carried the gleaming cup on her back. Like they do with babies, and other very precious things. And this time, not taking the trouble to walk by herself.

When we arrived in our village, she entered our compound to show the cup to my mother before going to give it back to the headmaster.

Oh, grown-ups are so strange. Nana is right now carrying me on her knee, and crying softly. Muttering, muttering, muttering that: '*saa*, thin legs can also be useful . . . thin legs can also be useful . . .' that 'even though some legs don't have much meat on them, to carry hips . . . they can run. Thin legs can run . . . then who knows? . . .'

I don't know too much about such things. But that's how I was feeling and thinking all along. That surely, one should be able to do other things with legs as well as have them because they can support hips that make babies. Except that I was afraid of saying that sort of thing aloud. Because someone would have told me never, never, but NEVER to repeat such words. Or else, they would have laughed so much at what I'd said, they would have cried.

It's much better this way. To have acted it out to show them, although I could not have planned it.

As for my mother, she has been speechless as usual.

MELISSA TANDIWE MYAMBO
Deciduous Gazettes

I didn't hate her at all. Just like I didn't hate Irene. Some say it is our tradition. It is our culture.

Not long ago, Irene had come to me on a hot, still Saturday afternoon to ask permission to go out with her friend, Tendai. They wanted to go to Turtle's afternoon session and promised to be back by five. They said they were going to listen to the music: soul, ragga, R & B, as if I knew exactly what that was. And dance.

How can you dance in those skirts, I had wanted to know, because they were so short, so skimpy, they barely covered their underwear. Red panties were peeping out.

They looked at me stonily as if I was the one who was mad. I tried all methods to discourage them; men will harass you, the street kids will follow you – whistling and berating you – you shouldn't expose so much flesh, it's not decent, the police may arrest you ... Finally, just as I quenched the thirst of surprise visitors with the water I kept in the fridge, I fortified myself by leaning on my old *ndonga*,[1] and said, 'It's not our culture, girls.'

They laughed and giggled and said, 'Yes, it is, Auntie!' And they ran to their school bags and brought out their history text-books, pointing at illustrations of nineteenth-century Ma-Karanga and MaNdebele women, bare-breasted and clothed in two square pieces of fabric joined by a cord that barely covered their pelvises and left much of their buttocks exposed.

[1] Walking stick.

14

Their words condensed into a shimmering rainbow, sliding them out the door and slipping them over my dam wall.

No, I didn't hate her, nor Irene. They were the same after all. Some say it is our culture.

◆

One day in the supermarket, I had seen Tete out of the corner of my eye, standing at the meat counter choosing rump steaks to feed her husband and children. Normally, I did not shop in Avondale because it was too dangerous, there was any amount of acting to be done just to purchase a few necessities. My body went slightly rigid but I am an experienced professional now and not by the flicker of an eyelid nor the tilt of my head could she tell that I had caught her staring at me. This time last year, she would have come up behind me, pinched my arm and when I turned, slapped her palm into mine – friendly, familiar, family.

If you divorce a man, does that mean Tete becomes an ex?

Today, I quickly moved along the aisle containing crisps and sweets and disappeared into the spaghetti sauces. There is a tacit agreement between us to avoid each other if at all possible. Why should we put ourselves through the ritual of respectful greetings, feigning pleased surprise and mutual delight at this chance encounter? The words will flow but the body will jerk awkwardly, the pupils oscillate at an extremely high speed and each of us will push our shopping carts in front of us – between us – defensively.

So we pretend not to see each other. But it is a more honest sort of pretence.

◆

Saru just sniffed and said, '*Uyu! Anobika mapoto. Ava, ka. Vachapedezerana.*'[2]

But people say she is young and pretty; others, that she is dark with a hard face and a mannish figure. Those who tend to claim she is unattractive are those who genuinely care for me. Wishing to comfort me, to console me, they condemn her as ugly – '*Akashata! Maiwe!* she's so dark, *kana pasi pebodo pari nani!*'[3] Why do my people still do this, I wonder, isn't it bad enough that whites censure our colour? Now we too must do the same thing. Or perhaps we always did it.

I don't know if this tradition of linking lightness and beauty started in 1890 or long before that. Some say we always found the milk-washed complexions of the BaTswana and the Sotho alluring. I don't know. But I do know that she is supposed to be half Tswana and not one of the Kalanga-speaking, darker-skinned people. It's not Ambi she's using or any other product, it's natural.

Her name is Lerato; they tell me it means love in her language. So, despite what my friends say, I am sure that she is attractive. I, too, find fair people more attractive even though Saru tells me I'm a victim of self-hatred, another colonial casualty. Saru says that black people despise themselves, like women, but that is another topic, a political subject, when I am talking about my hurt. My injuries. I know in my heart that she is pretty and voluptuous and has seductive breasts and sensual buttocks.

Perhaps I am just torturing myself but at least I can say it aloud now. When I first heard, I was at a kitchen party. I was looking very smart in a flowing lemon-yellow dress with matching shoes. Saru, home on holiday, was sporting a royal-purple Nigerian caftan with rich, gold embroidery dec-

[2] 'This one! She's a *mapoto* wife. They will resolve it between themselves.'
[3] 'Ugly! My! . . . The bottom of the pot is better than her.'

orating the front. We had arrived laughing, bearing gifts for the bride-to-be and were looking forward to an afternoon of raunchy gossip, belly laughs and drinking. It was Saturday afternoon, so there was plenty of time to recover from our gaiety in time for church the next morning. On that day, however, the fun hadn't lasted long at all.

No sooner had we deposited our gifts on the dining-room table than I excused myself to go to the lavatory. There was already a queue, and in front of me stood two ladies I had never seen before, both well-dressed and recently retouched. The catchy melody of Thomas Mapfumo's 'Vatete' was fading out and Dolly Parton had just begun to sing, 'My mistakes are no worse than yours, just because I'm a woman . . .' when they began speaking in low, confidential tones. Despite the music, I caught every splashy syllable of every last word.

'I believe the official Mrs Ncube is coming and so is Amainini,' said the one in powder-blue.

'You lie!' said her friend in green and white. 'Will they recognize each other? Does Mrs Ncube even know what's going on?'

'Mainini definitely knows what Maiguru looks like but as for Maiguru . . . Don't they always say, wives are the last to know?'

I quietly crept away, retreating down the corridor in search of Saru. She saw by my eyes and the damp chill surrounding me that something was wrong and we left, without a single goodbye, shrouded in silence.

The mantle of quiet quavered in my ears. It appeared so loud: a descant, a crescendo; but at least it blocked out the words and attempted to keep me dry and to deny the rest.

◆

My friend, Saru, told me to marry a white man, 'Perhaps these problems you're having will disappear.' But she warned, '*Manakira kure mvura yemubvumbi*.'[4]

Saru is not a hypocrite and had long ago followed her own advice. She lives in Frankfurt with a middle-aged Austrian professor of economics. No children but two cats; Saru concentrates on herself. She sells Shona sculpture to German art galleries and plans her buying trips for the European winter. Now, she just flits into town as and when she pleases. When she is there or here, she hums to Nina Simone and closes her eyes to Ambuya Stella Chiweshe.

Long and wiry with a hard, sharp face full of planes and shadows. Enormous, narrow hands and feet. Her eyes are a shade lighter than her skin. A witch's.

Sarudzayi is a staunch Christian. She says that she takes her faith more seriously than others and lives by the word of God. Adultery is a terrible sin, she says, when committed by a man or a woman. Then she quotes from the Book of Proverbs: 'When there were no depths, I was brought forth; when there were no fountains abounding with water. Before the mountains were settled, before the hills was I brought forth.'

When I wavered, it was she who said five words that washed away my weakness, 'Do you remember Mrs Mandaza?'

And I did, of course. Mrs Mandaza – beaten by her husband every Saturday night. Black and blue, as they say. When she heard about his mistress, she had in turn gone to the woman's house and beaten her. Blacker and bluer. Shortly after that incident, she had joined the Gracious Women's Fellowship.

Now we are two, Saru and Hannah – the white man's wife who is addicted to nicotine and navigating controversy and the

---

[4] 'Dirty water looks clear from a distance.'

18

pathetic divorcee who left her husband for no legitimate reason.

Women are married: we do not marry. Women are thrown out: we do not leave.

People are scared of Sarudzayi because she often strides into the unsaid – shamelessly and sardonically.

Meandering along, I asked her what I should say; how I should approach this; how I should apologize or explain to my brother; Irene was so young – what if she should fall pregnant; what if she doesn't listen to me; what if . . . ? Normally, we 'Attack' the girl, not the sugar daddy; 'Blame' the other woman, not the husband; 'Castigate' the daughter-in-law, not the son.

Saru stared at me, amber lights glowing in her eyes, 'Go and talk to the man.'

◆

My niece, Irene, came home from school today, ragged and sweaty, her uniform crumpled and dirtied. As soon as I looked at her, I saw that sunlight was trapped like fire in her eyes: they carried a secret which blazed out across the room and transformed the moment into theatre. The children were seated in front of the television, freshly bathed and hungry, anxiously awaiting Sisi Irene who should have started cooking at least forty-five minutes ago. I was also opposite the TV, wrinkled and worn out from a long day at the office, just recovering from the latest ZESA bill, when my young niece threw fire at me with her eyes and the drama began.

There are many levels of human communication but, unfortunately, most of us only choose to acknowledge verbal interactions.

In this moment, my niece was speaking to me, shouting at

19

me, screaming her secret soundlessly with her fire eyes. The children did not feel the heat emanating from her because it flowed from a spring beyond their years and experience, a hotness spitting with the sizzle of secret sex and the hiss of hidden happenings. Irene was magnificent as she stood there, at once trembling with excitement, dignified in her defiance and desperately frightened that I would ask her why she was so late coming home from school.

The benefit of communication beyond the narrow stream of words is that you can, if you so choose, ignore what you have understood, perceived, sensed and thus bypass the rugged mountains and the treacherous valleys.

Imagine you are at a play. It is a one-man act; a long, drawn-out soliloquy; the actor is talking out loud but feigning inner thought. He is pretending that you are not there and you permit him to do this. You are complaisant. You do not disturb the action of the play by allowing the reality of its falsity to intrude. You do not step on stage and strike up a conversation with him, although any member of the audience can do this, could do it, and hence violate the pact you have all made – to pretend. That is normal life: everyone makes believe that what is actually going on is the drama unfolding on stage; everyone senses, although at varying degrees of consciousness, that all the action is backstage and in the audience, but most of us are too frightened to test or threaten the fragility of the performance's innate falsehood.

I, too, am a coward. So I reneged. The flames scorched my throat, my breasts, my womb, my thighs. Yet I doused the blaze with my stream of words.

'Hello, Irene. You better prepare the dinner, the children are hungry. The chicken is defrosting on the sink.'

Irene obeyed my request, of course, but left me with the cindery odour of wet ashes and charred remains. I turned back to the television programme to watch other people play-acting.

◆

The official Mr Ncube didn't like Saru at all. He once described her as a 'loose firecracker'. In fact, he despised her because he was in total awe of her unconventional personality and her uncompromising spirit. He constantly complained about her reckless smoking in public; her disregard for womanly dignity; he doubted whether she was legally married. What kind of a woman, if she is natural, normal, does not produce offspring? The word 'whore' was scratching his throat but he didn't spit it out because he feared her.

He was jealous of her way with words: Saru had a very direct relationship with speech and utilized it as a blunt but effective tool to bludgeon home her meaning. It was only her lack of malice that saved her from offending the majority of people she came into contact with, although at the very least, she always caused discomfort and embarrassment and only sometimes antagonism and hostility.

One time, the official Mr Ncube insisted on taking us to a certain Mr Anderson's house for sundowners. Mr Ncube hoped to do business with Mr Anderson and this was the next step in the negotiations, so Saru and I clambered into Mr Ncube's Mercedes Benz and were whizzed off to Colne Valley. This was the day that Saru embarrassed Mr Ncube beyond redemption and it marked the demise of their forced courtesy.

The house was a Cape Dutch colonial-style mansion, painted a warm cream colour with chocolate-brown detail on the scalloped Dutch gables, affording a view of a whole hectare of illegally-watered luscious green lawn. This was during a severe drought but you would never have known it looking at the sparkling swimming pool, partly shaded by a glorious jacaranda tree, nestling next to the tennis court bordered by luxuriant flower beds, all bathed rosy-gold in the late afternoon sun.

There were about thirty people there, mainly whites with a sprinkling of blacks. Everyone spoke very gaily in high, nasal tones about the lack of rainfall, the PTC's delays in installing phones, sports, and private schools' escalating fees. It was very merry; the ladies drank Malawi shandies and club specials or brandies and coke while the men helped themselves to Zambezis or 'Shumbas' or something slightly harder. Except for Saru, resplendent in a shimmering white damask creation with a matching headdress, who slugged back straight scotch – no soda, no ice.

Saru's way with words was not affected by her drinking so there was really no excuse for what she said that day.

Mr Anderson was introducing his family to all the guests, taking them around to small clusters of people. His wife was fit from all her tennis-playing and had a ruddy, glowing complexion spoiled by thin lips which were pressed together as if to closely guard her true feelings. His daughter, on the other hand, possessed an ethereal beauty with her flowing blonde hair and eyes bluer than the sky. Yet she was so wan and thin, and like a cat, swishing its tail in agitation, nervously flipped her hair from side to side with her right hand while perpetually dragging on a cigarette with the left. As Mr Anderson finished presenting his child to Saru, he made an inadvertent comment. His daughter, he airily informed the general gathering at large in his flat Rhodesian accent, had just returned from an exhibition at Gallery Delta mounted by one of these newly-discovered, up-and-coming African artists.

'What is an African in your sense of the word?' said Saru,

quietly, dangerously, like a river that suddenly runs deep. There was a trickle of nervous laughter. Her cigarette tip glowed in the deepening twilight shadows.

'Oh, I'm sorry. What is the expression that you people prefer these days? At any rate, it was one of these young, black chaps – awfully good, I hear, trained overseas, I believe . . .' his words trailed off like a rivulet strangled by reeds. Some hummed, others averted their eyes and allowed them to dwell on the flower beds. They pretended.

'Where are you from, Mr Anderson?'

'Well, of course, I was born in Rhodesia but I'm a Zimbab-wee-an now.'

'Isn't "Zimbabwee" in Africa?'

◆

As the official Mrs Ncube, I should have gone home after that, after the kitchen party. I had access to the official residence after all, but how could I go there, seclude myself, retreat into the master bedroom that I shared with him? I couldn't speak because words seemed too dangerous, and Saru was driving, but I couldn't open my mouth to tell her where to go.

We sped along Harare Drive until we reached the gates but I just shook my head dumbly. Saru, mercifully, understood and quickly reversed. We took a short-cut through downtown Harare – the city flickered past so quickly – crossed through the industrial sites until we reached Highfields. I knew then that we were going to her sister's place in Machipisa because only the oldest boy was left at home. Everyone else had gone *kumusha*[5] for the weekend. I alighted from the passenger seat with my head bowed and left it to Saru to call out greetings to

---

[5] Home in the rural areas.

the neighbours. We were still dressed smartly from the kitchen party and driving Saru's imported Audi, so there were many curious eyes spilling over us as Saru let us into the house. It was dark inside, and I just managed to sit myself down on one of the two armchairs, placed side by side, because suddenly my eyes were blinded with hot salty tears.

Saru busied herself with the paraffin stove in the small kitchen adjacent to the lounge and I heard her swearing as she burnt herself with a match. The whole house filled up with the pungent odour of paraffin and I felt that if my scalding tears spilled down my cheeks they would ignite the atmosphere and I would, thankfully, erupt in a bluish burst of flame. But I wasn't consumed by fire although the tears flooded down my cheeks, mingling with the silence until the hush became a rushing, whooshing sound like rapids breaking against rocks. Saru handed me milky, sweet tea in a chipped enamel mug and sat down beside me in the other armchair, her doleful eyes staring straight ahead at a white cloth which announced in crooked letters, hand embroidered in bright green thread: 'Home is where the hart is.' Heart was misspelt.

We sat like that in the dark until dusk gathered at the doorstep.

◆

I am longing for the rainy season, for mulberries and *mazhanje*,[6] *nyimo*[7] and mangoes. But it is hot and dry, the clouds gather and threaten in the sky, hanging low over the city – but nothing, not even a drop. The earth is thirsty and the soil is powdery or packed down, desiring the deluge that

[6] The fruit of the *mazhanje* tree.
[7] Round nuts.

will signal the start of the planting season in the city's *vleis*[8] and the rural areas. This is primarily an agricultural country; we are dictated to by the whims of the soil and the vagaries of the seasons.

A gleaming silver BMW glides along the street and stops in front of our entrance. I am looking down from the third storey, but even from this height I recognize Irene as she jumps out – lightly, a little girl skipping in the park across the road, as if she didn't bear the burden of this double life.

Sometimes if you hear older people reminiscing – those born long before Independence and who lived mostly in Rhodesia – you might think that long ago we didn't have these problems. Today, the newspapers are filled with stories of rape, child sexual abuse and molestation. These problems existed then as they do now, but how to sort them out? Who will admonish them? Who dares punish them? Do we ever confront the culprits or just chastise the victims? And the line is blurring between these two categories like determining the water level during drought.

Words without the weight of authority behind them pass like dry, hot October winds through long grass and do not even stir the branches or challenge the trunk of a stubborn tree. Our children live up high, suspended in tree-houses furnished with the latest R & B music videos, ragga CDs, video games and a far-away look in their eyes – gazing, dreaming, wishing in the direction of America. They are preparing for flight.

Whilst we stretch our legs out in front of us on the prickly grass, fold our hands in our laps and look to the soil to sprout answers. We call upon the past and *vadzimu*[9] to provide guidance but these are forces of the earth. If Michael Jordan swept through and slam-dunked some advice to our youth –

[8] Marshy land.
[9] Spirits.

on morals and codes of behaviour – he would have much more luck than *vatete*.[10]

I hear her steps clanging on the iron fire escape and then pattering in the corridor, fumbling for the key and swinging open the door, giggling to herself – breathless, bubbling, bursting with news. She does not expect to find me back from work so early and drops her school bag in the hall by the phone. She picks up the receiver and dials:

'Tendai, please ... Tendai! He invited me to England! Do you think he's being serious? What should I tell her, Tete? I don't even have a passport ...'

I step out from the shadowy sitting-room and look at her ... looking at me ... the light fades from her face ... the fire from her eyes ... her mouth sags open ... she leans against the wall.

◆

My young niece is going out with a married man. A sugar daddy. This is the behind-the-scenes drama I have refused to acknowledge. Now, the smoke parches my throat, bringing stinging tears to my eyes, my nostrils are smarting and my hair singed.

Irene is smouldering like a charcoal fire, spitting yellow-red flaming sparks, dangerous enough to set me alight.

I found the new shoes first, led to them by the expensive aroma of genuine leather and shoe polish. They were pushed under the bed into the far corner by the wall in the room she shares with Tsungi; imported, mahogany-coloured with a block wooden heel, a size too small for her. Under them was a picture of Grace, radiant in her wedding gown, ripped out of *Parade*.

[10] Auntie.

26

Inside was a stub from the cinema and a silver chain with a pendant in the shape of a heart.

In the bathroom, I found diminutive bottles of shower gel and shampoo from the Monomatapa Hotel, the kind left in rooms for the guests.

In the kitchen, I found a dark-green box with 'Nandos' scrawled across the top in blaring red letters, and the remains of expensive lemon chicken and a few vinegar-soaked chips.

They did not want me to live alone with two children. How can a woman live alone? They sent Irene. As a cook, a babysitter, a chaperone. Another person in my tiny flat, another body in my cramped space. And in return, I promised my brother I would use the bits of my salary and my maintenance money to send her to school to complete her 'A' levels at a good school in town.

Now what type of education is this?

◆

I hugged my protective blanket of silence around me for seven days. I moved in a dreamscape, mechanically going about my day's business, sprinkling words like a *n'anga*[11] to chase evil spirits away. I greeted Mr Ncube in the morning; I prepared the children for school, dropped them off, went to work, came home from the office and cooked the evening meal, flipping, flicking words in all directions that dried quickly like a mid-afternoon drizzle. No one noticed anything out of the ordinary. They didn't remark that I saw them through a fog, they didn't recognize that my eyes were misted over. From that day I couldn't bring myself to speak his name, or call him Baba

---

[11] Spirit medium/traditional healer.

Tsungayi or even Baba. In my head, he became the official Mr Ncube.

Also, I didn't hear a single utterance during that week nor did I go to church. I went to work. I moved around his large, spacious house, my former home, and I looked for the clues that my mind was trying to shy away from, rebelling against the truth that had been there – smoking, fuming, smouldering – for a while. That's why I fled the kitchen party: I couldn't be faced with indisputable, living, breathing human evidence. I couldn't. So, I forced my mind to look for the inanimate traces – Mr Ncube's missing clothes. Where had he left his faded green corduroy sports jacket or his grey and red striped tie? The initials L.M. casually scrawled on his chequebook stubs for the amounts of a thousand, two thousand, sometimes five. He was late home and had lost his appetite. He was tired, worn-out and often overslept. Before, in a previous lifetime, he used to jump out of bed at five every morning.

How had I not seen this? But of course, I had sensed it yet resisted putting it into words – even inside my own head. Words can ambush you or drown you.

I eventually arrived home that night, to his big house with his enormous garden and his massive cars. I didn't know what to do or say but Mr Ncube assumed I'd had a bit too much to drink at the party, coerced by Saru of course, and rolled back over to sleep. I stripped, carefully placing my dress in the washing basket, and lay down beside my husband. I didn't wash or brush my teeth, I just lay naked on the cool sheets and listened to the nocturnal chorus of crickets outside the window, the neighbours' dogs barking, the occasional whirr of a passing car. He was breathing deeply and I listened to my husband, the father of my children, inhale, exhale . . . He was at peace.

But for me, his breathing filled, intoxicated, polluted my

lungs, my blood, my heart and my head every day for seven days until a great rushing wave of words tumbled out, vomited from my intestines, breaking over his head.

Some words sink deep into the ground, below the water table.

◆

Saru extracted the information from her – somehow, some way, in that brief, terse way of hers. Saru didn't believe in undercurrents. All I was told was his name and where he worked, and then Saru looked directly at me with her eloquent eyes and I knew what I was supposed to do.

But you can't just barge into someone's office, accuse them of an assortment of sins and then swan out? Can you? My first instinct was to ask a man, a relative, to do this for me but how could I explain the situation without exposing Irene to the family's wrath? I was not handling this the done way at all. What was the done way? Is the done thing? My thoughts were unspoken but ripples filtered across my eyes and into the stillness of Sunday afternoon. Saru spoke. She said:

'Hannah, my friend, did I ever tell you about the Africans in Frankfurt? There are many Africans in Europe these days, from all over the continent, but Hans is particularly fond of the West Africans, the North Africans, the Muslims. One day, he came home with an Algerian, a Senegalese and a Malian – countries you and I have never seen. They, all four men, sat down and began to discuss the Islamic faith and whether it was oppressive to women. All four sat and agreed it wasn't, that Islam cherished and respected women and basically the Quran was very even-handed, fair, just in dealing with men's and women's issues. According to the Quran, a man may take up to four wives. All four men vociferously discussed the value and historical reasons for this tradition. Then my fellow Africans turned to me and said: "How do you do it in Zimbabwe?"

'I looked at each of them, glowing with the exertion of intellectual exercise, and I told them this: "In Zimbabwe, it is the inverse situation. One woman may marry up to eight men." They were completely taken aback, nausea flitted across their faces, their hands trembled with self-righteousness and they sputtered out simultaneously: "But how do you know who the father of the child is?" said one. "That is filthy. One woman cannot sleep with so many men. It's disgusting," said the other, and the third: "Whose surname does the child take?"

'Calmly, I explained that we did not mind who the father of the child was: all my husbands would live together in harmony and nurture that child who would, naturally, take my family name, as did my husbands. We, I stated clearly, did not think of this as filthy but it was our tradition, our culture, our heritage – any woman who had the economic means was able, if she so wished, to take up to eight husbands.

"But how will the man know which child he has fathered?" said one. "Every African man wants to have a child he knows for sure is his."

"No man would put up with such a situation. It's unnatural," said the other, and the third: "What kind of men are these that can stand for such shocking behaviour? Are they real men?"

'I clarified the situation, patiently illustrating that to us there was no significance in who had *fathered* the child. All that was important was who his mother was – after all, any sperm can impregnate a woman, but only the woman can bear the child. Therefore, all the husbands rejoice when their wife falls pregnant and the child is born into a loving family of caring fathers. They are each his father because no one knows who the biological parent is. Furthermore, I expanded on my theory: no woman will put up with even the slightest infidelity on the part of any of her husbands.

'Finally, I reminded them that no man, anywhere in the world, could ever be certain beyond the shadow of a doubt that a child was his; only a woman has that privilege.

'Throughout this entire exchange, Hans sat in stunned silence, staring at me as if the scales had fallen from his eyes. After his friends had left, shaking their heads and muttering to themselves in disgusted impotence at the barbaric, uncivilized ways of Southern Africa, Hans asked me why I had lied like that. I simply told him, "I am tired." '

◆

Our climate has changed. We used to have a very precise rainy season and we learned in school that heat built up throughout the day, mid-afternoon cumulonimbus clouds would form and then a quick, heavy downfall that would last for about an hour and that would be the end of it. The sky washed white and the fresh scent of rain on soil.

For the last few years though, the rainy season has mutated. It's cloudy all day long and it drizzles, like England. We are not yet used to this type of rain. Some attribute it to global warming, others claim it has religious significance, but me, or should I say I, I don't know what it is. We still have thunder and lightning storms and some say powerful *n'angas* can direct a lightning bolt towards a certain person or house. But I come with water on my tongue, hotness in the palm of my hand and mountains and valleys hidden in my heart.

'My name is Hannah Ncube. We don't know each other and I'm very sorry to have disturbed you without an appointment. I have a problem, Mr Kanyangarara, I believe your first name is Fidelis. What does the name mean? Does it have something to do with the word "fidelity"? How ironic. You see, my husband was cheating on me. With another woman. I know what it feels like. It hurts.'

It is October and we are waiting for the rains.

'You know, I was lucky though. I always put my own pay cheque into my own bank account. So when I left, it was difficult to say goodbye to such a big house and all the comfort my husband's money bought us but . . . I don't know, maybe I spent too long with the missionaries but I couldn't. I couldn't live with that. So when I left, I was fortunate that I had always kept my own account. Not all women keep their own money; many give it to their husbands, you know. I can pay for the rent of a small flat and his company pays for the children's school fees, of course, but I pay for Irene's with my own salary. I've always been a firm believer in education. Many blame the way I've turned out on my education so you'll excuse me, won't you, if I appear a bit unorthodox?'

A raindrop sliding down a glass pane collects dust and when a sun ray catches it, there is a rainbow trapped inside. Refracted. Reflected.

It is October and we are waiting for the rains. It is hot.

'What are you doing with my niece, Mr Kanyangarara?' Abruptly, I hurl the accusation from my stone fortress on the mountain top. Words of fire and ice. I am in charge of this production. I don't want to mess it up.

But he is far below me, huddling behind his desk. Outside his large window, the purple jacaranda flowers are silently dropping in the heat until they reach the baking pavement or the melting tarmac and they are sizzled, roasted, broiled a bruised brown.

'Nothing at all, Mrs Ncube, nothing. This is a . . . misunderstanding . . .' I look deep into his eyes and he feels the heat, perspiration trickles down his forehead and he shifts in his chair, puts a finger inside his collar under the knot of his tie, gagging.

'If you don't put an end to this "misunderstanding", I warn you the consequences will be very grave indeed. I will tell your wife.' I take a deep breath, filling my lungs to capacity and then exhale, sharply, through my mouth, knocking him over with a strong mountain wind pregnant with rain. 'I will tell your wife and your children. I will sue your family for damages. I will whisper in your colleagues' ears. I will exaggerate, embellish, elaborate the story – she is pregnant, the risk of HIV, she is fourteen not seventeen. I will lie to shame you because I hold you responsible. You are an adult, a married man, a father. She is an adolescent, a girl, a child. How dare you?'

I am breathing the thin air at the very top, the atmosphere that produces light-headedness – I can fly away.

But he, him, the culprit, he is cowering: a drowning rat trying to cling on to a slimy, slippery stone before he is carried away again by another flood. Terror soaks through him: it emanates from the pulse beating rapidly in his neck and the hands clinging to his collar, desperately trying to allow himself air. What is suffocating him, I wonder, is it water or smoke?

He wrinkles in the hot water. He is burnt out like cold white ash. He will not bother me any more.

◆

Mai Sithole follows him to *her* flat in Strathaven. She sits in her car the entire night, parked in front of Block C, fogging up the windows and breathing in her own carbon dioxide. When he comes out at half-past six the next morning, dressed and ready for work, she watches him get into his car, start up the engine and leave. At quarter to seven *she* comes out, elegant except for her *Bata takkies*[12] that she has put on to walk to the ET stop. Her fake-leather handbag is slung over her shoulder and in her right hand she carries a TM plastic bag, out of which her office stilettos peep. At half-past seven the domestic worker arrives, she retrieves the key from under the doormat and lets herself in.

Mai Sithole sits in her car, perspiring. Towards twelve, the domestic worker emerges, carefully hides the key behind the potted plant adjacent to the door, calls to her friend next door, '*Sisi, ndakuenda kumashops*',[13] and then jauntily proceeds on her way.

Mai Sithole waits five minutes, gasping in the still air, steps out of her car, recovers the key from its hiding place, unlocks the door and slips in. The radio has been left on. She raises the volume; it is Tsitsi Mawarire's talk-show programme, they are discussing the issue of polygamy, traditional versus modern perspectives.

Mai Sithole picks up the telephone table and smashes it into the television screen. There is a mirror over the dining-room table. She picks up a chair and throws it into her reflection again and again until shards of glass slide to the floor in jagged geometrical shapes: triangles, pentagons, octagons. She drags the chair into the kitchen and hurls it into the stove. Then she picks up a meat cleaver and hacks at the electric cables leading from the oven to the wall. She puts the stopper in the sink and turns on the taps, the hot and the cold, full blast. She heaves against the refrigerator, raggedly dragging gulps of air into her lungs. When it is about half a metre from the wall, she attacks it with the knife; air escapes from the coils of cable, exhaling.

[12] Canvas lace-up shoes.
[13] 'Sisi, I'm going to the shops.' ('Sisi' is an affectionate term for an older sister.)

Mai Sithole moves to the bedroom, wheezing with her exertions, removes her underwear and climbs up on to the bed. She opens her legs wide and urinates on to the duvet. She takes her knife and slits through the bedclothes, deep into the mattress until the stuffing puffs out. She empties the closets of all clothes: men's wear, ladies' suits, gym gear, lingerie, and dumps them on the bed. She takes a match and lights one corner of one of the three pillows. She places the burning pillow on the heap of clothes.

She enters the bathroom, places the stoppers in the bathtub and sink, turns the taps to full. She opens the medicine cabinet and flings the contents into the swirling water. She retrieves a half-used lipstick, ruby red, and writes vertically down the full-length mirror behind the door in large capitals, HURE.[14] Then she retraces her steps to the lounge, picks up the tape deck, still airing the views of phone-in callers, rips the cord from the wall plug, places the now silent machine gently on the floor and puts her foot through each speaker.

Mai Sithole opens the door, panting gently, locks it behind her and tosses the key across the car park into the hedge. She steps into her car, opens the windows wide to let in some fresh air, reverses and drives away.

Mrs Phiri swallows the information down with her *sadza* and *Lacto*.[15] She looks at her friend, Mrs Ndlovu, sideways. They sing together in the church choir. She says, 'You're lying. You're just jealous. What do you want with my husband? Why are you creating these problems between us?' She stands up from the table, walks to the kitchen sink and turns the tap on

[14] Prostitute.
[15] *Sadza* is a porridge made from maize meal and *Lacto* is powdered milk.

with her left hand. Under the stream of tepid water, she carefully rubs the *sadza* from her palm, her fingers, from under her nails. Closing the tap leaves only silence in the kitchen except for the hum of the fridge and the deep freeze. Gathering up her groceries, Mrs Phiri lets herself out and walks through the gate to her house next door. Mrs Ndlovu finishes her meal in stifling solitude.

Mr Phiri is late coming home. In fact, he has not come for supper since last Wednesday. So Mrs Phiri takes up her ironing, sits and lets the fog stay in her brain so that she remains numb. The television flickers in front of her eyes as her right arm sweeps back and forth – with special attention to collars and seams – over his shirts, his trousers, his underwear. She refuses to think, she refuses to remember backwards or dream forwards. Instead of sitting warm, heavy, comforting, familiar, in her stomach, the *sadza* feels like a stone, an undigested lump. She inhales, exhales, vomits up her insides, respires, expires. She breathes but the fog stays, saturating her lungs with water droplets until she coughs and sputters, a deep, wet, racking bark like a hyena's cackle. The children disappear to bed, one by one, and she sits through the sitcom, the programme line-up, the feature, the adverts, the epilogue. A Christian 'thought' to sleep on; transmission is over. The screen goes blank, then fuzzy, and finally bands of colour streak down the screen. In the lower left-hand corner the time flashes in digital numerals – 00:41:23. As the seconds flicker into the future, she stares ahead at the screen.

Mr Phiri unlocks the door and is surprised to find the light on in the sitting-room. Mumbling to himself he fumbles for the light switch and jumps when he sees his wife looking at him. He had thought she was a witch because his senses are hazy with alcohol. For this reason he doesn't see the fog glowing grey behind her pupils. She greets him respectfully, '*Makadii enyu, Baba? Maswera sei ko, Baba?*[16] They repair to their bedroom. He soon passes out, snoring loudly. She lays back in her cloud and drifts away. He wakes up the next morning before she does. He washes, he shaves, he dresses, he awaits his tea. Mrs Phiri lies in bed, her muscles light like mist. He grows hungry, his stomach grumbles for porridge because beer has left it hollow. She explains she is unwell, her head feels weightless, it is full of rain clouds. 'But I will cook dinner tonight. Come home for curried chicken tonight. I will cook, but now, I must rest.'

Mrs Phiri doesn't do the housework, she lies in all day. Towards the evening, she rises and sets to work in the kitchen, defrosting chicken, his favourite pieces only. She chops onions and tomatoes for soup. As the chicken boils, she slips into her bedroom, opens the drawer of the dressing-table. Underneath the flimsy underwear and petticoats she feels for the little bag. Inside the plastic, twisted and tied at the neck, is a smaller round bundle wrapped in newspaper. Returning to the kitchen, she opens the small parcel, pinches the powder between her fingers and sprinkles it lightly in the chicken broth. Lastly, she cooks *sadza* to the texture he prefers, using *upfu*[17] sent by his mother.

Mr Phiri is at the door, she hears his key in the lock, and bends to take out the plates from the cupboard. On the counter lies this month's *Horizon* magazine. On the outside cover is a picture of a woman opening the door to her husband arriving home from work late in the afternoon. Two children run joyfully to meet him. The slogan across the top is, '*Hapana muphuwira unopfuura Chibataura.*'[18] He enters her kitchen and he finds her leaning against the fridge door, holding her

[16] 'How are you, father? Have you had a good day?'
[17] Mealie meal.
[18] 'There is no love potion better than *sadza*.'

womb and bent over double, laughing her cough, coughing her laugh.

Mai Celestina goes straight to her, their, bed and she lies there – unwashed, unkempt, unmoving. For days, the curtains are drawn. She refuses to eat; they say she is ill. She does not speak a word, her eyes stare through him, the concerned children, curious relatives, inquisitive visitors. She cannot hear them but the sound of the toilet flushing abrades her abdomen, the banging of pots in the kitchen chafes her chest, and the worried whispering of the children grates, rasps, chips, files away at the aura of quiet enveloping her. She lies in bed – unblinking, unhinged, unwell, . . .

Then one day, he comes and informs her that he is making it official, she must accept her, call her Mainini, she is pregnant and he has already begun the traditional proceedings to make her his wife.

Mai Celestina lets his words in one by one, one every few seconds, hours, days . . . until they take form in her head and she dreams pictures – herself with another man, revenge, sweet vengeance, reverse jealousy, he is betrayed, he is the cuckold. She lies there – unfulfilled, unsatisfied, unhappy.

Then one day she gets up out of her bed and goes to wash. She spends a long time cleaning herself up, rubbing lotion into her dry skin, massaging oil into her knotted hair. She sits down and eats, gobbles down her food, devouring great quantities. Speech tumbles off her tongue, grown thick and mossy, and she jokes with the neighbours and teases the children.

Mai Celestina is not afraid of confrontation now. Silence is replaced with garrulousness. Words are no longer a threat. In fact, she has heard he bought a new stove for Mainini: she wants one too, plus a fridge. Mainini is dressed smartly in a new dress from Truworths: she wants one too, plus shoes from Edgars. Mainini has a domestic: she wants one too, plus a sewing machine.

But Mai Celestina still sometimes lies on her bed – unthinking, unfeeling, unemotional.

◆

Words can trap you. You must tread carefully, especially with those who drop them carelessly from their mouths and do not know the value of silences during conversation. Those who do not pause in their speech are usually trying to ensnare you and do not wish to hear what you might say, in case it dams their waterfall before you have been washed away. Beware.

Babamukuru came to call me one evening without warning and began talking before I had even completely opened the door. The next thing I knew I was being carried along in a fast current, rushing downstream over rocks in a thundering wave, until I reached a quiet pool and clambered ashore, only to discover I was sitting in his house opposite Ambuya who had come all the way from Gwanda to dilute me with her opinion.

'Why, my child, have you done this to my son?'

I made the mistake of thinking it was a question and I took advantage of the pause to dip into my inner reserves, to fortify myself from my secret spring. I attempted to get my bearings, looking around the plush room furnished entirely in Adam Bede oak. Doilies crocheted by Ambuya adorned every possible surface, the headrests of each and every red chintz armchair and sofa, the coffee table, the TV cabinet. My own flat was also full of her doilies even though I'd been giving them away as gifts for years. There was a copper clock above the fireplace in the shape of the map of Zimbabwe with the Victoria Falls blazing down one side, captured in eternal motionless wonder by the metal mould. A tusk of ornately carved ivory stood guard at the entrance to the dining-room. Babamukuru's house smelt of Cobra floor wax and boiled chicken. These impressions flitted through my mind in a few seconds. I took for granted that I still had some time to gather my thoughts, I assumed she would move like water in a well as is the habit of those who are older and wiser. I was wrong. She was far too crafty and wound-up for that and, realising she was allowing me time to shore myself up against her onslaught, she opened her mouth and poured down on me like a thunderstorm in the middle of winter.

'How could you do this to my son, Mai Tsungayi?'

The intricate web of words wormed their way into my mind, despite myself, whispering their ransom price. It was sticky, and I kept finding myself glued to her explanations, caught in their borders, pinned down by their weight, strangling, suffocating. The ransom I had to pay was my backstage pass and my seat in the audience, after which I would become a full-time actress – at which point she would release my abducted status as a respectable woman. Once upon a time I would have done just that, but my husband, her son, that man called Solomon Mandla Tafadzwa Ncube, had broken a part of me. I think it was the desire to play-act that he destroyed, and since then the tributaries of speech have held little interest for me and I have retreated to the mountain tops.

But Ambuya's words were threatening to snatch me off my perch and drown me because they were weighed with the words of my mother, my sister, my auntie. They were the words of women, of a woman, whom I used to love. How is it, I wondered, that I am now the accused, I am the one who must defend myself, I am the one on trial? Is that a trick of speech? Or a dramatic technique? A change in climate? She doesn't know I'm no longer in the actors' guild.

'Where is your son at this moment, Ambuya?'

Her eyes grew weary and her shoulders sagged. I had interrupted her flow of speech. I could see she was tired.

'Where is your son now, Ambuya?'

The trickle of water seeping away sang in my ears and the cool, fresh mountain breeze rushed into my eyes joyfully.

'Mbuya, your son is with his mistress. Should I really take the blame for his infidelity? Should I suffer every night, sharing a bed with a man who can look me in the eye and lie to me, unblinking? Should I be expected to cook his food and iron his shirts while he gallivants around town with his mistress, for the honour of being called Mrs Ncube? Should I?

'For years, Ambuya, you cried to me that your husband had continuously embarrassed you, persistently humiliated you with his steady stream of girlfriends. How many children does he have and with how many women? We still don't know and oh, how you suffered his adulteries, one after the other. You have told me many times.

'Now, how have you raised a son who can do the same thing, blindly following in the footsteps of his father? How have you brought up a son who can treat another woman so badly? Who can do to me what his father did to you? How can you accept in the son what repulsed you in the father? How could you let a house be built twice with unstable foundations?

'If you cannot hold him responsible for his mistakes, then it is not I who will take the blame. It is you. If you cannot reproach him for his wrongs, then bear his guilt yourself. Do not blame me for your son's choices.

'I will not pretend I have not seen what I have seen.'

Words when they climb ashore and run rampant over thick

bush, through which no path has ever been cut, or trample territory where you must remove your shoes, can murder and assassinate. They can cut and gash, sinking deep into the lower intestines until the dark-red blood spurts out, like a spring, and soaks you in the pungent odours of digested foodstuffs and bowel movements and makes you sweat from the sheer heat. Beware!

Because I knew this and had learnt respect for my elders, I asked one question – eight words – and allowed silence to reap what she had sown.

Babamukuru found us hushed and still and delivered me to my door: he is muted, speechless.

◆

I don't hate her at all. Nor Irene nor Lerato. They are the same after all. Some say it is our tradition. It is our culture.

LINDSEY COLLEN

The Enigma

'I don't want anything to happen to you,' Marie's father said.

With this, he walked out of her room into the only other room in the house: his room which doubled as the lounge.

He made this percussion sound as he went, shaking the house-key and his taxi-key on the dodo keyring in one hand and at the same time shaking coins around in his trouser pocket with the other hand.

Her homework was lying heavy on her desk in front of her. An essay title: 'One thing I can't stand' sat there resentfully.

'Nothing will happen to me, father,' Marie answered.

On the inside cover of her exercise book, she quickly wrote the word 'unfortunately' in a strange handwriting. Then, just as quickly, she rubbed it out so hard she nearly made a hole in the thing.

'Airport,' he added, 'I've got a client for the airport.'

'That's good, father. That's lucky. Beginning the day with a good trip.'

As he went out, he locked her in. She saw a wasp fly out just in time.

She looked out of her window as if to fly off herself.

Marie suddenly found words coming out of her mouth. She mumbled them to herself: 'The family reduced to father and daughter'. Like an essay title.

Then, out aloud, she said: 'Father and daughter and keys and money.'

She shivered. Her own words scared her.

43

'Must stop talking to myself,' she thought. 'After all he's been through to bring me up.'

'Father and daughter and keys and money.' The thought came back by itself. She was cross with it. Vexed.

'Anyway, there's something missing in it,' she thought.

But she couldn't for the life of her think what it was.

'Maybe it's that stupid dodo on the keyring,' she thought. But of course it wasn't that.

'*One thing I can't stand.*' Marie sighed like a girl can only sigh when looking at a blank page with an essay title at the top of it.

'I can't stand waiting to be proposed to,' she thought.

Suddenly she remembered the fifth thing in their family.

That was it: *Father, daughter, keys, money and waiting for a request for her hand in marriage.*

Hand. As if dismembered, was it? Or, as though if she got her hand snared, she could, in due course, be pulled in and caught?

She started her essay: 'My father is waiting for someone to make a request for my hand in marriage. This is one thing I can't stand. When I hear the two words *bon garçon*,[1] I feel the anger . . .'

Marie thinks of his car. 'Wake up to it in the morning. School uniform on, front door. I take two steps, only two small steps, over the cobbled stone pavement under the mango branches in that inviting rich outdoor air. Then there I am, inside it. The car door closing in on me.

'On the way, we pass my classmates. Walking. Yes, swinging their arms. In the open air. In flocks. They shriek. They throw their school bags in the air and catch them. They take short cuts. They stop at the tobacconist's and buy pickled cucumber

---

[1] A 'suitable boy'.

and put salt on it and eat it right out there in the sun. The wind makes their hair stand out electric.

'My father's car drops me at the school gate. Again I walk two paces, small paces, as if my feet were bound, over those few cobbles outside Eden College. The street for two seconds expands like the universe on two sides of me.

'Vertigo.

'Then into the corridor. Gone. He drives off.'

But she doesn't write all this down. She writes: 'My father thinks that this is why I need an education. To get a *bon garçon* from a good family, who's got a good job.'

'Is there going to be a beginning, a middle and an end in my essay?' she thinks.

Uninvited, the car comes back into Marie's thought. It's when the last bell rings. The others jumble out into the streets, running, laughing, high-pitched howling. She gets to the front gate, and there it is. The car. Door already open.

Impaled.

Impaled by gratitude that she has a father who loves her so much that she doesn't even have to walk about in the two o'clock sun.

'I can't stand the waiting for a proposal. It makes me think of my faults. Although I've never walked barefoot, my feet are cracked. My hair is dry and I've got split ends. There are mango stains on my right hand.'

These thoughts jumble around inside her head.

All gone now. Marie quakes. She quietly pulls the bit of paper, a receipt of some sort, out of her desk drawer. She has been waiting to get it out. Her name, her age: seventeen years. Her secret. Has something happened to her?

The result of the test. She reads quickly. She knew all along anyway. Yes. There it is, in writing: 'Positive'. The word 'positive' has so many meanings.

She feels the lashing she'll get, already. Her father and the belt.

She sees school receding. The thought horrifies her. She knows the confinement to a convent, like a prison that will face her. She feels the ostracism in all their eyes. The stares at mass.

And yet.

An enigma: She feels she's stopped the waiting.

One act. And something is happening now.

Life is growing inside her and will, in due course, be visible to everyone. In public. In front of her friends and teachers. Everyone. Her father will be faced with the fact.

It will be her family now.

'The family reduced to mother and child.' She mumbles this to herself now. She smiles. More keys at the convent. She hears their sound already. And she has no money to rattle.

But at least there's no more waiting for her hand to be asked for in marriage.

Her essay is left unfinished.

FARIDA KARODIA

The Red Velvet Dress

The face of the pale, wasted figure, inert on the hospital bed, is barely recognizable. I watch from the window as my aunt, teary-eyed, fusses with the bed-covers, smoothing them, folding back the sheet, caressing the bony hand on the counterpane. The fingers on the right hand are loosely curled – except for the rigid, unyielding index finger, frozen in a gesture of accusation.

I turn away from that image to gaze out at the small patch of garden. An elderly woman, in hospital gown and slippers, slowly and painfully inches her way across the lawn. A door closes down the hall and out of the silence I hear the approaching squelch of crêpe soles on rubber tiles.

The nursing sister enters the ward and smiles reassuringly as she addresses Tante. 'Your sister has surprised us all, hasn't she, Mrs de Wet?' Her tone is calm and clinical as she studies my mother's chart.

'One sometimes wonders just how much a poor body can take. It's been one thing after another. We didn't hold out much hope for her. Not with the way the cancer has spread. But there you are, she's still with us. It's out of our hands now.'

Tante inclines her head towards me. 'Sister, this is Wilhelmina's daughter, Katrina.'

The sister's glance leaps between us, then, nodding absently, she says, 'Well, I'll leave the two of you, then. Good day, Mrs de Wet.' Her eyes dart back to me before she sweeps out of the room.

◆

The last time I saw my mother was twenty-five years ago. It was the final day of my trial and she was standing outside the courthouse watching me as I shuffled towards the waiting van, hands and feet shackled.

For a brief instant our glances locked. Then she was gone. Swallowed in the crowd. There are few recollections about that day, except vague impressions of people, voices, the flutter of the judge's red robes and the dust churned up by traffic. The numbness had already set in by the time I entered the cell to start my sentence.

Now, three months after my release from prison, and in response to my aunt's urgent summons, I am at my mother's bedside as she slowly slips away.

The sun's rays catch my mother's hair, webbed across the pillow like strands of gossamer. Her scalp is smooth and pink beneath those fine wisps. My childhood memory is of my mother with a full head of auburn hair, plaited and pinned to the top of her head like a crown.

Tante still fusses. She is ten years older than my mother, but with the illness having wasted my mother, Tante now looks more like the younger sibling. My fingers gingerly reach out to touch the strands of hair spread on the pillowcase.

'She lost much of it when the cancer started,' Tante says. 'I wrote to you about it.'

Tante was the only one who had kept in touch with me. She was the only one who had believed that Pa had done all those unspeakable things I had accused him of.

'Katrina, I know that in her heart she has forgiven you.'

'Has she ever mentioned my name?' I ask.

Tante shakes her head and drops her glance.

I study my mother's still face. I desperately want to feel love or remorse, but there is only this cold emptiness inside me.

On that long drive to prison I had exhausted my tears. I had emptied my soul. The familiar stab of rage returns as I remember the years I spent in prison, hoping and praying for word from her. No word ever came. There was just the silence which stretched between us like a taut wire, quivering with anger and condemnation.

My mother's jaw trembles and a gurgle rumbles deep inside her chest like an awakening volcano. Startled, we listen, but Ma's breathing again settles into a quiet rhythm.

Memories come flooding back.

Pa had called me *Katjie* – Kitten, a derivation of my name, Katrina. It was a name he used when we were alone together. A name I grew to despise. Later, at school, my classmates corrupted it to *Katjie Kleurling* – Coloured Kitten, a derogatory tag.

The third label: 'Killer', came later.

It was on everyone's lips after my arrest, reminding me of what I had done. I needed no reminder. I would take the image of my father's shocked expression to my grave – his look of horror as I raised the barrel and pulled the trigger.

Tante's voice breaks into my thoughts, '*Kom*, Katrina. Let's go home. We'll come back later. There's nothing we can do now. Wilhelmina doesn't even know we're here.'

I follow Tante out of the room, pausing in the doorway to glance back at the figure on the bed.

'What you need is a good home-cooked meal,' she says. 'Look at you. You're all skin and bone.'

I am so exhausted. Even the slightest movement seems to require enormous effort.

At the house Tante drags a comfortable chair out onto the stoep for me and then goes into the kitchen. I lean back in the chair trying to find peace, but there is none. Memories and regrets flood my thoughts. I struggle to get away, but the past envelops me like a dark, damp mist.

Tante returns and joins me on the stoep. She pulls the other chair up closer, takes my hand and quietly speaks to me about the Christian virtue of forgiveness.

The cold emptiness still grips me and I have nothing to say. After a long silence between us, Tante goes back into the kitchen to prepare tea. I remain outside, alone and totally overwhelmed. My head pounds. It feels as if nails have been driven into my skull. I squeeze my eyes shut, shrinking into the darkness where I have always found refuge. But today there is no sanctuary from my terror. The darkness is filled with demons beating their wings inside my head. Out of this evil darkness a familiar refrain surfaces. At first muffled and distant, it becomes louder, more persistent until it drowns out all else.

'*Katjie Kleurling . . . Katjie Kleurling.*' The chant mesmerizes me. The monotony of the refrain traps me. I am eight years old again.

'*Katjie Kleurling . . . Vieslike leerling!*'[1] Bessie Grobbelaar sings out at the top of her voice as Hanna and Elsie turn the skipping-rope.

'*Vieslike Kleurling!*' The phrase 'Filthy Coloured' rings in my ears long after the rope has stopped turning. The rejection of my classmates is agonizing.

There is little consolation for me in Ma's assurance that her great-great grandparents had arrived with the second wave of Dutch settlers, and that her great-great aunt was Katrina van der Walt.

'*Katjie Liefling . . . Katjie Liefling . . .*'

At first Pa used to call me *Katjie Liefling* – Darling Kitten. I was only five years old and I thought he loved me.

The skipping-rope turns faster. Bessie ducks, skips in, jumps to twenty-five and skips out.

[1] 'Awful student'.

I watch from the edge of the playing field, fists tightly balled, knuckles white and bloodless, heart pounding with murderous fury. Suddenly there is an explosion in my head and I tear into their midst, lashing out wildly, legs snarling in the rope. They scream in mock terror and run off laughing and screeching, '*Mal Katjie! Mal Katjie!*' Crazy Kitten.

Blinded by angry tears, I stumble away, falling on the rutted footpath. Their shrill voices follow me, adding to my humiliation.

Some of them have run out of abusive words, but a few voices still chant, '*Kroeskop! Kroeskop!*' The disparaging reference to my hair is a bitter reminder that I am not one of THEM. My hand reaches up to smooth back the hair that pokes from my head like clumps of dried straw.

Face down on the ground, I smell the earth dampened by my tears.

◆

Sounds from the kitchen rouse me from the past. My eyes open on sunlight glinting off a garden tool. The sweet aroma of freshly baked bread fills the air. I am touched by the way Tante fusses about me. I can't remember anyone ever doing anything special for me. My only recollection of Ma is that of disciplinarian: a dispenser of punishment and pain.

My mother was a rigid, uncompromising woman whose very existence was defined by the precepts of her religion. There were times when it seemed almost as though Ma had hated me from the moment I was born. Yet, at other times, in flashes, I saw the two of us together, her warmth wrapped around me like a summer's breath.

It is hard to decide from hindsight exactly when she changed.

Perhaps I was mistaken and there was never anything between us. After all, I had always been an outsider: my coarse hair and dark skin, anomalies amongst the blonde hair and blue eyes of our community. At church I could feel those blue eyes following me, boring through me. It never ceased to amaze me how the congregation, with their narrow resentful eyes, lips tightly pursed in disapproval, were able to pry them open in order to praise the Lord.

Sometimes I thought my mother deliberately inflicted pain on me. In the mornings the torturous routine of combing my hair left me in tears, my mother's knees firmly locked round me to keep me from wriggling out of her clutches as she tried to undo the snarls.

Nellie, who was my trusted friend, perhaps the only friend I ever had, agreed to help rid me of the source of my misery – my hair.

Nellie's father, Piet, a coloured labourer, worked on our farm and her mother, Anna, worked in our kitchen. Nellie was four years older than I, but we had grown up together, sharing a history that went back to infancy.

Using the sheepshears in the barn we clipped off all my hair. Ma found me like this: my hair sheared off, my scalp as white and as bald as the bottom of a new-born lamb.

Nellie started howling, begging for mercy even before the strap my mother had brought out had touched her. When my turn came, I sobbed quietly, each lash falling on my bare buttocks with blistering accuracy.

'*Katjie Kleurling* . . .'

◆

I gaze out over Tante's patch of back-garden. A green plastic hose snakes through the dusty flower beds. At the end of the hose a sprinkler snaps back and forth, spraying arcs of water on the sun-baked earth.

The scene reminds me of the drought we had that one year when I was about eleven years old. It was the worst in decades. Sheep were dying in their hundreds. The pathetic bleating of the lambs as they succumbed was more than any of us could stand.

Half the farmers in the district had been bankrupted by the drought, and Pa wasn't coming home much any more. Ma must have already known about Nellie. Later, of course, it became common knowledge that Pa had fathered Nellie's child. I had many reasons to hate my father then already, not only for what he was doing to me, but to Nellie also.

The night Nellie's father died, Pa had come home with an injured arm. The next morning a gang of workers found Piet's body lying near the fence. That afternoon Pa went into town to report the theft of several of his sheep. He stayed away all afternoon, ostensibly visiting with the minister Dominee Faurie and the sergeant of police. In the end the police report about Piet's death concluded that he had been killed by thieves.

I will never forget the look on Anna's face when she came to the house after Piet's funeral. She knew that Piet had died at Pa's hands. Ma tried in every way to show her small kindnesses, but Anna had slammed the door shut on us.

Piet's unexpected death not only meant the loss of a loved one, but it also shifted the extra burden of supporting the entire family onto Anna's shoulders. Pa never uttered a single word to her. Not one word of sympathy or regret issued from his mouth. He went about his business as though nothing had happened.

Four years later Anna told us that Nellie was pregnant again. Pa chased Anna, the pregnant Nellie and her child off the farm. Later that same day, Pa instructed me to ride out into the veld with Johannes who had to track a jackal that had taken two of the lambs. I took along Pa's shotgun and was about halfway across the field when a labourer caught up with us and told us that Nellie had hanged herself from the willow tree. Pa must have been told too because he and I arrived at the willow tree at about the same time.

There was not a flicker of emotion in my father's steely eyes as he gazed at the body, soft green fronds wrapped around Nellie's head like a crocheted shroud.

I got off my horse and, with the assistance of two labourers, cut Nellie down. Pa got off his horse and walked away to gaze out over the veld. It was probably at that precise moment that something snapped inside me.

I picked up the gun, dropped earlier in my haste to cut Nellie down, and blinded by a red haze of hatred and rage, raised the gun and pointed it at my father. He heard the click of the safety catch being released and turned. The blast caught him about three-quarters of the way through his rotation, the impact throwing him off balance.

◆

Tante comes onto the stoep, carrying a small, enamelled tray. Startled out of my reflections I sit up, taking the tray with its pattern of yellow tulips from her. 'I brought us some tea,' she says. 'Don't get up.' She waves me back into the chair. 'When your mother dies, there'll be some money. It rightfully belongs to you and I'll see to it that you get it.'

Tante pauses as she pours the tea and looks directly into my eyes. 'I think your mother knows that you're here. She should have gone a long time ago, but I believe she hung on long enough for you to come.'

From her apron pocket, Tante takes an envelope. 'Wilhelmina made me promise that I'd give you this after her death, but I think you should have it now.'

I take the envelope tentatively, turning it over in my hands. 'Go ahead,' Tante urges. 'Open it.'

I slit the envelope. Folded inside a sheet of blank writing paper is a faded photograph.

I recognize it instantly. It is a picture of me at the age of four, wearing a red velvet dress with a crocheted collar. Stunned, I gaze at the image in the picture. Dear God! I had searched through piles of old photographs, trying to find evidence of this scene.

'This is the picture, Tante! I remember so clearly the day we took this picture!'

Although I had a clear recollection of this scene, my mother always claimed I had imagined it. For almost my entire life, the image of the red velvet dress, imagined or real, with its white lace collar, had been with me. The dress is the clearest memory I have of my early childhood.

The picture is black and white and as I scrutinize it, it acquires colour and texture. 'Look, Tante, you can't see the colour, but this was the red velvet dress I told you about. There is the crocheted collar! I remember the park also. All those golden leaves on the ground crunching under our feet . . .'

Tante's gaze slowly moves from my face to the photograph.

'That's me,' I say again. I sit forward now, animatedly pointing out features in the picture. 'You can't see the others.' The adults had been cut off at the waist. 'But I know that's Ma and Pa holding my hands.'

I was skipping between them, the camera capturing my joy.

Dear God. Why had Ma tormented me so? I sink back into the chair. This photo is a memory I had cherished through the darkest days of my life. The sun had streamed through the trees that day, burnishing the thick carpet of leaves. To me, this picture was proof that I had at one time enjoyed a normal relationship with my parents.

The phone rings. Tante gets up out of her chair. She pauses in the doorway, her gaze full of sympathetic understanding. I wait, sensing that she has more to tell me. She ignores the ringing telephone. There is a look of desperate urgency in her eyes. She has something important to say, but the shrill ringing of the telephone persists.

'That man in the photograph with you and Wilhelmina is not your father, Andries Marais. It is a man by the name of Hendrik Tobias – a coloured,' she says. 'He was your mother's lover.'

Shocked, I gaze at her. The phone is still ringing. The sound seems to come from a long distance, as though it has travelled through a vacuum. Suddenly it stops.

'When Andries found out about this coloured man, he went crazy. He almost killed Wilhelmina. He was going to leave her. He had known all along that you were not his child. I mean even an idiot could see that you were different. Your mother explained it away by saying that you were a throwback to one of our ancestors. He might have accepted your mother's story; after all, it had happened in other Afrikaner families, but . . . then . . . your mother became careless and one day he found her with her coloured lover. You were about four years old at the time.

'Your grandfather, fearing the scandal and the disgrace to the family name, paid off all Andries' debts. It was only when he had paid off the farm that Andries agreed to stay on. No one except the immediate family knew about this arrangement. A few months later Hendrik Tobias was murdered. The police never found his killer.' She pauses for a moment – a moment which seems to stretch into eternity.

The phone began to ring again.

'So now you know Andries Marais was not your real father. Ag . . . I'd better go answer that telephone.'

She turns away impatiently and goes into the house.

In a stupor, I absently watch two flies buzz around the sugar pot.

Tante returns. 'That was the hospital.'

I get up out of the chair, stiff-jointed, thinking about what Tante has told me. She puts out a restraining hand.

'Sit. There's no need to hurry any more.'

I sit down again and pick up the photograph.

'There was a time when your mother was full of life and fun. Andries Marais soured her.'

Tante gathers the flare of her skirt in a bunch between her knees and, with a sigh of weary resignation, sits down heavily. '*Nou ja*, let's finish our tea and then we can go to the hospital. Wilhelmina has passed on,' she says, her eyes brimming with tears.

She reaches for the dishcloth lying on the ground beside her chair and expertly flicks it just above the sugar pot. Stunned, the two flies fall to the ground.

NORMA KITSON

Uncle Bunty

You could have said Uncle Bunty was the ideal husband: he was a good provider. You couldn't say he was the perfect father though because by the time he and Auntie Betty's third child was born, I suppose Uncle Bunty was rather sick of kids.

Elvis, their first, was a black-haired dream child: obedient, solid, a tough little boy; and Suzy, who came two years later, was a pretty curly-haired little girl. No objections. But Cole was a challenge to any South African dad raised on the macho-milk of racism, sexism, ageism and every other ism you can think of that said 'a man's a man' in the climate of 1940s Durban in South Africa.

Cole played with dolls from an early age, tripped rather than walked and had a decidedly girlish touch about him. This is probably what drove Uncle Bunty to decorate his bathroom, loo, shower room, walls, floors – his whole personal ablution block and dressing suite – with a hardy linoleum-type black-and-white paper (or paper-type linoleum) depicting thousands of women's breasts, or perhaps the same pair reproduced – I've forgotten which. I think having tits around made Uncle Bunty feel somehow safe.

After Cole was born there was a remarkable change in Uncle Bunty. He assumed a stoop and was often seen to chew on his wild black moustache. Not all the shoutings, beatings and objections, footballs, motor-cars or other boy-toys had the slightest effect on Cole. He wore Suzy's dresses at the touch of a button, gazed into his own brown eyes in every mirror in the house, straightening his eyebrows and flicking up, wherever possible, his paternally-controlled short hair. The parenting skill Uncle Bunty used to the full was bullying to thwart Cole's natural tendencies, convinced he could make a 'man' of him.

Uncle Bunty was a private in the South African army when he met Auntie Betty serving soup to soldiers at the Durban Jewish Club during the Second World War. Auntie Betty was at a nervous stage of her life: her four older sisters were married and now the youngest, Tookie, was about to tie the knot with Izzy. So, although she was only twenty years old, she was going to miss the boat and be called an old maid or some other choice appellation reserved for dogs who couldn't get a bloke.

Auntie Betty had a good look around her before she settled on Bunty, but there was nothing for it. No man of her dreams emerged and he would have to do. Everyone warned her he was a philanderer and even though she clutched onto her precious virginity, it was doubtful whether she would ever actually get him under the *chupah*.[1] So after he had shone his eyes at her a couple of times, Grandpa David stepped in to manage the affair. In time-honoured fashion he sat in his big red leather-studded chair behind the expanse of his enormous shiny stinkwood desk in his study while Bunty tried to maintain his aura of casual manliness, but twisting his neck, relieving the tightness of his shirt collar every now and then, showing terrible tension. He was not feeling casual. He was bloody scared of the old man and could not understand why he had been summoned. He did not have long to wait.

'So vhat you doing mit mine second-yongest den? You having yourself a good time mit mine dochter, or vhat?'

Uncle Bunty quivered slightly and half lowered himself, expecting to be invited to sit for this important meeting. But no invitation was offered. He straightened his back, bent both

---

[1] The canopy the bride and groom stand under in a Jewish wedding.

his knees to get his balls into place and sucked in his lower lip so that his thick black moustache swept his upper chin.

'Well, it's a bit early for all that, isn't it? I mean I've only known Betty such a short while. We going out, getting to know each other . . . you know.' He looked nervously at the wooden face of the old man and added: 'She's a wonderful girl.'

'Early! Vhat's early aboud it? For how long you want footsie-tootsie with mine dochter before you pop de kvestshun, huh? Vhat you vaiting for? A vonderful gel, nu? Vhat more you vant?'

There were a few more exchanges of this nature and then Grandpa David did ask Bunty to sit down and the real business began. If Bunty would go the whole hog – marriage – he would receive a passage out of the army, a hotel on the beach front and a monthly means of survival.

From the minute they were married, Auntie Betty's face in repose assumed a strange mixture of relief and horror. This made her look permanently worried. For the first ten or so years she was terrified of her husband. He blustered, shouted, ordered, directed; had loud, crude opinions about everything – and particularly about Betty's responsibility for the effeminacy of their son, Cole. It was her fault. It was all her fault.

Like many macho-men, Uncle Bunty was a womanizer. While Grandpa David was alive, this activity was kept in check, or at least under the lap. But after the old man died, Uncle Bunty usually wore a woman on his arm, a perpetual grin on his smug face, not actually flaunting but also not really attempting to hide his activities, secure in the knowledge that he was viewed as a great all-round success. His voice got even louder and his opinions more raucous.

That's when Auntie Betty went all spiritual. I think she felt that probably the after-life had more to offer than the present one. She spent her afternoons at séances and tarot readings and was not surprised when a fortune-teller let her into the secret that the tall dark man in her life was not adding to her happiness.

'Akshully,' she said quite calmly, 'I hate him.'

It was the first time she had made such an admission even to herself, and she went to a gynaecologist and had her tubes tied.

It was common knowledge that Uncle Bunty had to have a 'girl' on his arm at the casinos, the races, playing poker or just lolling at the reception desk of his hotel or up in his private suite. They were known by the hotel staff and the family as his 'secretaries'. In the incredible heat of Durban, no one turned a hair when Uncle Bunty, after exchanging a few words and sucking on his moustache, handed over to his Indian hotel manager and 'went to take a shower', often hustling before him into the lift a blonde of one sort or another, looking as if she had sore feet and usually carrying a black patent-leather bag.

When the cousins, Minna and Billie, were playing draughts behind the settee in the lounge of the Mediterranean villa Uncle Bunty had built in Vause Road, despite the drone of the piped *muzak* into every room of the house, they both heard Auntie Betty say to her sisters one tea-time: 'I don't care. *Reely!* I read a book where it said men who have to go after women like that aren't good at performance, and in Bunty's case that's a real fact. I never liked it, I don't miss it and I'm jolly glad he's got other women to do it with.'

It was an admission she must have regretted dearly because for months afterwards, whenever our aunties were together, in twos, threes or more, they remarked on how Auntie Betty didn't know what she was missing and how fantastic *their* husbands were at it and Minna told Billie she couldn't wait to find out for herself.

'You not going to just go and have sex with somebody, are you?' asked Billie.

'Oh, no – never!' said Minna. 'My mother would have a fit!

61

She says my hymen is my most precious possession. I'd be too scared, you know. You supposed to bleed on the sheet when you get married, otherwise he'll know you've had sex and never forgive you.'

'Don't you think it's unfair that men can?' asked Billie.

'Oh, no,' said Minna. 'Men are different. Doesn't your mother tell you about things? Men have got to have it. They different. If they don't get enough they make wars and things, you know, they get aggressive. They got to relieve themselves, like going to the lav, I suppose.'

'Well,' said Billie, 'my dad doesn't believe all that. He thinks there's nothing wrong with sex and that men and women are mostly the same with their feelings.'

'Oh,' said Minna, '*your* dad. Everyone knows he's wonky in the head with his ideas about everything. The other day I heard Auntie Pearl tell Auntie Bea she saw him on the stoep reading a book. When she asked him what it was he got all impatient and said: "This is a pamphlet by Dr Pixley Ka Isaka Seme about the state of this nation. Anything else you want to know, Pearl?"

'Pearl said. . .' Minna screwed up her face, trying to remember exactly. ' "You reading things written by a *black – a natiff?*" Auntie Bea looked so shocked that Auntie Pearl was pleased. "*Ja*," said Pearl. "I said to him, I said: I bet there's plenty books by decent white men you haven't read yet." Your dad just jumped out of his chair and slammed out and gave both aunties his real dirty look. Your dad's reelly funny, you know, Billie. He's just so different.'

Billie sucked in some air and looked away. She loved her father very much but she didn't know how to defend him against the attacks made by nearly every member of the family.

◆

Uncle Bunty was very good at making money. He soon had a string of hotels and he was much happier when, in their late teens, one by one, his three children went to live in America. Auntie Betty got thinner and thinner. She missed her children and it was many years before she nagged his consent to visit them. After that, in her sixties, she was seldom in Durban and she seemed much happier traipsing from Los Angeles to New York and then Chicago, visiting her adult children.

It was when she was cradling Isabel, Suzy's daughter, in her arms that the cable came from Durban.

'Return immediate. Bunty very ill. Love from your brother, Joe.'

'Oh tse!' is what Auntie Betty said. 'Well, he's 76, so he's bound to get sick from something or other, isn't he! I mean, he eats meat, traipses around at all hours, doesn't exercise. What did he expect?'

But she dutifully packed up and took the next plane back to Durban. Bunty had cancer and had to have his scrotum removed. Minna thought it was really funny and tripped around the furniture in her mother's lounge, chanting to Billie and Fenella:

> 'Uncle's health has much improved
> Since he's had his balls removed.
> Now bereft of his desire
> He stays at home, and pokes the fire.'

Billie and Fenella gazed at her with shocked faces. But fearless Minna just grinned back.

When Billie told her father he just said: 'Got his comeuppance. Well, he did, didn't he? Used his prick like a weapon and now it's falling off. Something religious about that – like the Second Coming.'

'What you mean, Dad?' asked Billie.

'Don't you worry about it, darling. It's just the chickens come home to roost, that's all.'

Uncle Bunty was very ill for a long time, but he recovered some of his strength. Auntie Betty stayed in Durban, nursing him, nursing also rage and frustration. In 1984 she even went to Uncle Joe to discuss getting a divorce.

'I've never loved him. We've been married now for over forty years. He's a terrible man. He's never read a book. He's a complete bully and now he's sick he wants me every minute. I never fancied him when he was well so why can't we just call it quits?'

Uncle Joe was horrified: 'You mean you vant to leave your husbin vhen he needs you, vhen he's so sick? Vhat! You outta your tiny mind or vhat? You'll bring todal disgrace on this fambly mit your rubbish. You go home, be a good gel, look after your husbin. I don't lissen to your crazy nonsince you silly gel.' And he gave her a fond smack on the bum and five hundred rand to buy a new dress.

Well, Uncle Joe was the law in our family so Auntie Betty continued to endure the suffering of looking after her husband. No more girlfriends. No days and nights at the hotels. Now Uncle Bunty stayed at home, sore, restless, complaining, discontented. His children each paid one dutiful visit to him from America and then they were gone.

Auntie Betty languished in her horrible duties, got even thinner, unhappier and even stopped wearing make-up and wedgies. For three years, this horrible situation continued. Then, one day, when Bunty was sitting in the garden sunning himself and Auntie Betty was picking up and stacking his comics and peeking into his magazines of pretty women wearing strings of black lacy threads round their waists and up their bumslits and nude women bending over so you could see their hair and everything down there and others with their big boobies standing up – you'd never know how – the telephone next to his bed rang. Auntie Betty reached over: 'Hello?'

'Can I speak to Bunty, please?'

'Who is calling?'

'It's Melly here. Who's that?'

'This is Betty here.'

'Oh, well. Are you the nurse or something? Can I speak to Bunty, please.'

'Well, he's in the garden at the moment. Can I give him a message?'

'Yes, please. If you will. Just tell him Freddie is really ill and I know it is difficult for Bunty, but Freddie really wants to see him about some shares or something. He says it's urgent. Our grandson insisted I phone and tell Bunty, even though I'm not supposed to use this number. Please call him for me. It's his wife speaking.'

That's how Auntie Betty learned that Uncle Bunty had a whole other family in Durban (a wife and three sons, all real males) and how, at the age of 81, she got her divorce from Uncle Bunty and lives very happily now in her flat overlooking the Durban beach front and goes to America whenever she feels like it.

VERONIQUE TADJO

The Betrayal

One day, a woman and a man who loved each other intensely decided to have a child.

'We cannot live this way without sharing some of our blood,' said the woman. 'I want our love to become flesh.'

'This child will be the carrier of hope, I am sure,' agreed the man with a nod. 'We will teach him everything we know.'

The next day, the woman was pregnant. Before the day was over, she had given birth to a son.

Then the man cried: 'Love has won! We have created life! Our son will be our messenger.'

Father and mother remained close to the child teaching him to love and to have faith. They spoke to him constantly. The child listened.

'You will cross continents and meet many people. Tell them what we taught you. Rebuild the cities destroyed by violence and oppression. Let wild flowers grow freely and do not crush the clouds. Tell them about the water that never dries up. Dip your hands into the earth and breathe its smell and, above all, believe in yourself.'

When the child felt ready, he said goodbye to his parents and left without looking back. With each step he took away from them, he was visibly growing up. So much so, that by the time he could see the city in the distance, he was already a man.

Things were not easy for him. Everywhere he went, he saw nothing but despair. Though the city shimmered with lights and pleasures, if you took only one step away from the main road you could find mud and filth. People wore gold, but if you turned your head a little you could see street children and disabled people in rags. The roads were straight and lit by powerful lamps but, if you wanted to go further, you could inhale the dust of abandoned pathways.

But all this was nothing. The worst part was that people had lost faith. They spoke of freedom and of change, but these were empty words. No one believed in them. The northern wind could blow for weeks and dry people's skin, but the heat would return with greater intensity and stronger stench. People were drifting about, totally out of breath.

And him, what was he doing?

◆

He spent his days growing up and watching life go by. His eyes recorded everything. But in reality, he felt extremely cut off from others. Communication was so difficult that it became painful. What he was looking for always seemed to be elsewhere. At times, he wanted to leave the town, to go away in order to discover something else.

What was more, he could sense he had changed. Oh, not that much, but enough to recognize the difference in himself. He had to try hard not to abandon his beliefs and even though, in his dreams, he still saw his parents and heard their soft words, he also had powerful nightmares which left him without breath in the pit of the night. He had the feeling he was falling into space. His head throbbed and he was scared. He knew very well that this was anguish. And it was so thick and heavy, he could have held it in his hand.

Anguish was wrecking his life. It broke his spirit and stripped him of his strength.

'This has to stop,' he decided. 'This must end.'

◆

It was around that time he fell in love.

She had eyes shaped like cowries and her skin was the colour of sand. The city was in her gaze.

For her, time was no obstacle since she considered herself genderless. She was an undefined creature who was going through life half-heartedly and who couldn't care less if she wore a skirt and had pointed breasts.

Her life flowed regularly, and she knew how to take advantage of it. She just lived it. Love was a secondary notion, an awkward feeling. She thought she had too many things to do. Her innocence draped her in unparalleled elegance.

◆

Was that why she looked so beautiful? Was that why he wanted to possess her? He did not know. He only felt this great desire. Morning and evening, her scent had a perverting influence on him. It was a constant battle within him: at the same time, a denial and an acceptance of this passion which would not stop plaguing him.

She agreed to let him speak to her. She could sense in him a strange strength which she was lacking entirely. She sat listening to him while she was wrapping and unwrapping around her finger the white handkerchief her parents had given her. She knew that what he said was part of life, but she felt she wasn't ready for it. She still needed time. A lot of time. Possibly years.

◆

One evening, she drank from a glass he handed her. All of a sudden, the brightness of the lights seemed to crush her. She felt heavy. Her eyes closed.

And that was how he possessed her.

In the city, people became petrified. A thick silence laid over the night. Darkness deepened.

When she regained consciousness, she bore a child in her womb.

'I am dying,' she whispered. 'This child is not mine. He will bring unhappiness.'

Finally, he realized the magnitude of his betrayal and started to panic. He wanted to erase what had happened. He wanted to deny it. But her belly was enormous and as round as the earth. He placed his hand on her distended navel to find out if the child was still alive.

◆

All at once, there was a gigantic flash of lightning which jostled the clouds. The sky started to slip away and trees let out screams. At the same time, an unbearable heat descended. Smoke heavy with dust surrounded nature which burst into flames. A violent breath of air burned people and knocked down buildings. Skin pulled away in layers. Eyes dried up. Big tufts of hair fell out. Everyone died violently. Iron melted down and ran along the ground. The blazing horizon was carved into an enormous mushroom cloud.

Extract from 'As the Crow Flies' – an unpublished translation of *A Vol d'Oiseau*

LEILA ABOULELA

The Museum

At first Shadia was afraid to ask him for his notes. The earring made her afraid; the straight long hair that he tied up with a rubber band. She had never seen a man with an earring and such long hair. But then she had never known such cold, so much rain. His silver earring was the strangeness of the West, another culture shock. She stared at it during classes, her eyes straying from the white scribbles on the board. Most times she could hardly understand anything. Only the notation was familiar. But how did it all fit together? How did *this* formula lead to *this*? Her ignorance and the impending exams were horrors she wanted to escape. His long hair was a dull colour between yellow and brown. It reminded her of a doll she had when she was young. She had spent hours combing that doll's hair, stroking it. She had longed for such straight hair. When she went to Paradise she would have hair like that. When she ran it would fly behind her; if she bent her head down it would fall over her like silk and sweep the flowers on the grass. She watched his ponytail move as he wrote and then looked up at the board. She pictured her doll, vivid suddenly, after years, and felt sick that she was day-dreaming in class, not learning a thing.

The first days of term, when the classes started for the M.Sc. in Statistics, she was like someone tossed around by monstrous waves – battered, as she lost her way to the different lecture rooms, fumbled with the photocopying machine, could not find anything in the library. She could scarcely hear or eat or see. Her eyes bulged with fright, watered from the cold. The course required a certain background, a background she didn't have. So she floundered, she and the other African students, the two Turkish girls, and the men from Brunei. Asafa, the short, round-faced Ethiopian, said, in his grave voice – as this collection from the Third World whispered their anxieties in grim Scottish corridors, the girls in nervous giggles – 'Last year, last year a Nigerian on this very same course committed suicide. *Cut his wrists.*'

Us and them, she thought. The ones who would do well, the ones who would crawl and sweat and barely pass. Two predetermined groups. Asafa, generous and wise (he was the oldest), leaned over and whispered to Shadia: 'The Spanish girl is good. Very good.' His eyes bulged redder than Shadia's. He cushioned his fears every night in the university pub; she only cried. Their countries were next-door neighbours but he had never been to Sudan, and Shadia had never been to Ethiopia. 'But we meet in Aberdeen!' she had shrieked when this information was exchanged, giggling furiously. Collective fear had its euphoria.

'That boy Bryan,' said Asafa, 'is excellent.'

'The one with the earring?'

Asafa laughed and touched his own unadorned ear. 'The earring doesn't mean anything. He'll get the Distinction. He was an undergraduate here; got First Class Honours. That gives him an advantage. He knows all the lecturers, he knows the system.'

So the idea occurred to her of asking Bryan for the notes of his graduate year. If she strengthened her background in stochastic processes and time series, she would be better able to cope with the new material they were bombarded with every day. She watched him to judge if he was approachable. Next to the courteous Malaysian students, he was devoid of manners. He mumbled and slouched and did not speak with respect to the lecturers. He spoke to them as if they were his equals. And he did silly things. When he wanted to throw a piece of paper in the bin, he squashed it into a ball and aimed it at the bin. If he missed, he muttered under his breath. She thought that he was immature. But he was the only one who was sailing through the course.

The glossy handbook for overseas students had explained about the 'famous British reserve' and hinted that they should be grateful, things were worse further south, less 'hospitable'. In the cafeteria, drinking coffee with Asafa and the others, the picture of 'hospitable Scotland' was something different. Badr, the Malaysian, blinked and whispered, 'Yesterday our windows got smashed; my wife today is afraid to go out.'

'Thieves?' asked Shadia, her eyes wider than anyone else's.

'Racists,' said the Turkish girl, her lipstick chic, the word tripping out like silver, like ice.

Wisdom from Asafa, muted, before the collective silence: 'These people think they own the world . . .' and around them the aura of the dead Nigerian student. They were ashamed of that brother they had never seen. He had weakened, caved in. In the cafeteria, Bryan never sat with them. They never sat with him. He sat alone, sometimes reading the local paper. When Shadia walked in front of him he didn't smile. 'These people are strange . . . One day they greet you, the next day they don't . . .'

On Friday afternoon, as everyone was ready to leave the room after Linear Models, she gathered her courage and spoke to Bryan. He had spots on his chin and forehead, was taller than her, restless, as if he was in a hurry to go somewhere else. He put his calculator back in its case, his pen in his pocket. She asked him for his notes, and his blue eyes behind his glasses took on the blankest look she had ever seen in her life. What was all the surprise for? Did he think she was an insect? Was he surprised that she could speak?

A mumble for a reply, words strung together. So taken aback, he was. He pushed his chair back under the table with his foot.

'Pardon?'

He slowed down, separated each word, 'Ah'll have them for ye on Monday.'

'Thank you.' She spoke English better than he did! How pathetic. The whole of him was pathetic. He wore the same shirt every blessed day. Grey and white stripe.

◆

On the weekends, Shadia never went out of the halls and, unless someone telephoned long-distance from home, she spoke to no one. There was time to remember Thursday nights in Khartoum: a wedding to go to with Fareed, driving in his red Mercedes. Or the club with her sisters. Sitting by the pool drinking lemonade with ice, the waiters all dressed in white. Sometimes people swam at night, dived in the water – dark like the sky above. Here, in this country's weekend of Saturday and Sunday, Shadia washed her clothes and her hair. Her hair depressed her. The damp weather made it frizz up after she straightened it with hot tongs. So she had given up and now wore it in a bun all the time, tightly pulled back away from her face, the curls held down by pins and Vaseline Tonic. She didn't like this style, her corrugated hair, and in the mirror her eyes looked too large. The mirror in the public bathroom, at the end of the corridor to her room, had printed on it: 'This is the face of someone with HIV.' She had written about this mirror to her sister, something foreign and sensational like hail, and cars driving on the left. But she hadn't written that the mirror made her feel as if she had left her looks behind in Khartoum.

On the weekends, she made a list of the money she had spent: the sterling enough to keep a family alive back home. Yet she might fail her exams after all that expense, go back home empty-handed without a degree. Guilt was cold like the fog of this city. It came from everywhere. One day she forgot to pray in the morning. She reached the bus stop and then realized that she hadn't prayed. That morning folded out like the nightmare she sometimes had, of discovering that she had gone out into the street without any clothes.

In the evening, when she was staring at multi-dimensional scaling, the telephone in the hall rang. She ran to answer it. Fareed's cheerful greeting. 'Here, Shadia, Mama and the girls want to speak to you.' His mother's endearments: 'They say it's so cold where you are . . .'

Shadia was engaged to Fareed. Fareed was a package that came with the 7Up franchise, the paper factory, the big house he was building, his sisters and widowed mother. Shadia was going to marry them all. She was going to be happy and make her mother happy. Her mother deserved happiness after the misfortunes of her life. A husband who left her for another woman. Six girls to bring up. People felt sorry for her mother. Six girls to educate and marry off. But your Lord is generous: each of the girls, it was often said, was lovelier than the other. They were clever too: dentist, pharmacist, architect, and all with the best of manners.

'We are just back from looking at the house,' Fareed's turn again to talk. 'It's coming along fine, they're putting the tiles down . . .'

'That's good, that's good,' her voice strange from not talking to anyone all day.

'The bathroom suites. If I get them all the same colour for us and the girls and Mama, I could get them on a discount. Blue, the girls are in favour of blue,' his voice echoed from one continent to another. Miles and miles.

'Blue is nice. Yes, better get them all the same colour.'

He was building a block of flats, not a house. The ground-floor flat for his mother and the girls until they married, the first floor for him and Shadia. When Shadia had first got engaged to Fareed, he was the son of a rich man. A man with the franchise for 7Up and the paper factory which had a monopoly in ladies' sanitary towels. Fareed's sisters never had to buy sanitary towels, their house was abundant with boxes of *Pinky*, fresh from the production line. But Fareed's father died of an unexpected heart attack soon after the engagement party (five hundred guests at the Hilton). Now Shadia was going to marry the rich man himself. 'You are a lucky, lucky girl,' her mother had said, and Shadia had rubbed soap in her eyes so that Fareed would think she was weeping about his father's death.

There was no time to talk about her course on the telephone, no space for her anxieties. Fareed was not interested in her studies. He had said, 'I am very broad-minded to allow you to study abroad. Other men would not have put up with this . . .' It was her mother who was keen for her to study, to get a post-graduate degree from Britain and then have a career after she got married. 'This way,' her mother had said, 'you will have your in-laws' respect. They have money but you will have a degree. Don't end up like me. I left my education to marry your father and now . . .' Many conversations ended with her mother bitter; with her mother saying, 'No one suffers like I suffer,' and making Shadia droop. At night her mother sobbed in her sleep, noises that woke Shadia and her sisters.

No, on the long-distance line, there was no space for her worries. Talk about the Scottish weather. Picture Fareed, generously perspiring, his stomach straining the buttons of his shirt. Often she had nagged him to lose weight, without success. His mother's food was too good; his sisters were both overweight. On the long-distance line, listen to the Khartoum gossip as if listening to a radio play.

◆

On Monday, without saying anything, Bryan slid two folders across the table towards her as if he did not want to come near her, did not want to talk to her. She wanted to say, 'I won't take them till you hand them to me politely.' But smarting, she said, 'Thank you very much.' *She* had manners. *She* was well brought up.

Back in her room, at her desk, the clearest handwriting she had ever seen. Sparse on the pages, clean. Clear and rounded like a child's, the tidiest notes. She cried over them, wept for no reason. She cried until she wetted one of the pages, smudged the ink, blurred one of the formulas. She dabbed at it with a tissue but the paper flaked and became transparent. Should she apologize about the stain, say that she was drinking water, say that it was rain? Or should she just keep quiet, hope he wouldn't notice? She chided herself for all that concern. *He* wasn't concerned about wearing the same shirt every day. She was giving him too much attention thinking about him. He was just an immature and closed-in sort of character. He probably came from a small town, his parents were probably poor, low-class. In Khartoum, she never mixed with people like that. Her mother liked her to be friends with people who were higher up. How else were she and her sisters going to marry well? She must study the notes and stop crying over this boy's handwriting. His handwriting had nothing to do with her, nothing to do with her at all.

Understanding after not understanding is fog lifting, pictures swinging into focus, missing pieces slotting into place. It is fragments gelling, a sound vivid whole, a basis to build on. His notes were the knowledge she needed, the gap filled. She struggled through them, not skimming them with the carelessness of incomprehension, but taking them in, making them a part of her, until in the depth of concentration, in the late hours of the nights, she lost awareness of time and place, and at last, when she slept she became epsilon and gamma, and she became a variable, making her way through discrete space from state 'i' to state 'j'.

◆

It felt natural to talk to him. As if now that she had spent hours and days with his handwriting, she knew him in some way. She forgot the offence she had taken when he had slid his folders across the table to her, all the times he didn't say hello.

In the computer room, at the end of the Statistical Packages class, she went to him and said: 'Thanks for the notes. They are really good. I think I might not fail, after all. I might have a chance to pass.' Her eyes were dry from all the nights she had stayed up. She was tired and grateful.

He nodded and they spoke a little about the Poisson distribution, queuing theory. Everything was clear in his mind, his brain was a clear pane of glass where all the concepts were written out boldly and neatly. Today, he seemed more at ease talking to her, though he still shifted about from foot to foot, avoiding her eyes.

He said, 'Do ye want to go for a coffee?'

She looked up at him. He was tall and she was not used to speaking to people with blue eyes. Then she made a mistake. Perhaps because she had been up late last night, she made that mistake. Perhaps there were other reasons for that mistake. The mistake of shifting from one level to another.

She said, 'I don't like your earring.'

The expression in his eyes, a focusing, no longer shifting away. He lifted his hand to his ear and tugged the earring off. His earlobe without the silver looked red and scarred.

She giggled because she was afraid, because he wasn't smiling, wasn't saying anything. She covered her mouth with her hand then wiped her forehead and eyes. A mistake had been made and it was too late to go back. She plunged ahead, careless now, reckless, 'I don't like your long hair.'

He turned and walked away.

◆

The next morning, Multivariate Analysis, and she came in late, dishevelled from running and the rain. The professor, whose name she wasn't sure of (there were three who were Mc-something), smiled, unperturbed. All the lecturers were relaxed and urbane, in tweed jackets and polished shoes. Sometimes she wondered how the incoherent Bryan, if he did pursue an academic career, was going to transform himself into a professor like that. But it was none of her business.

Like most of the other students, she sat in the same seat in every class. Bryan sat a row ahead which was why she could always look at his hair. But he had cut it, there was no ponytail today! Just his neck and the collar of the grey and white striped shirt.

Notes to take down. *In discriminant analysis, a linear combination of variables serves as the basis for assigning cases to groups.*

She was made up of layers. Somewhere inside, deep inside, under the crust of vanity, in the untampered-with essence, she would glow and be in awe, and be humble and think, this is just for me, he cut his hair for me. But there were other layers, bolder, more to the surface. Giggling. Wanting to catch hold of a friend. Guess what? You wouldn't *believe* what this idiot did!

Find a weighted average of variables . . . The weights are estimated so that they result in the best separation between the groups.

After the class he came over and said very seriously, without a smile, 'Ah've cut my hair.'

A part of her hollered with laughter, sang: 'You stupid boy, you stupid boy, I can see that, can't I?'

She said, 'It looks nice.' She said the wrong thing and her face felt hot and she made herself look away so that she would not know his reaction. It was true though, he did look nice; he looked decent now.

◆

She should have said to Bryan, when they first held their coffee mugs in their hands and were searching for an empty table, 'Let's sit with Asafa and the others.' Mistakes follow mistakes. Across the cafeteria, the Turkish girl saw them together and raised her perfect eyebrows. Badr met Shadia's eyes and quickly looked away. Shadia looked at Bryan and he was different, different without the earring and the ponytail, transformed in some way. If he would put lemon juice on his spots . . . but it was none of her business. Maybe the boys who smashed Badr's windows looked like Bryan, but with fiercer eyes, no glasses. She must push him away from her. She must make him dislike her.

He asked her where she came from and when she replied, he said, 'Where's that?'

'Africa,' with sarcasm. 'Do you know where *that* is?'

His nose and cheeks under the rims of his glasses went red. Good, she thought, good. He will leave me now in peace.

He said, 'Ah know Sudan is in Africa, I meant where exactly in Africa.'

'North-east, south of Egypt. Where are *you* from?'

'Peterhead. It's north of here. By the sea.'

It was hard to believe that there was anything north of Aberdeen. It seemed to her that they were on the northern-most corner of the world. She knew better now than to imagine sun-tanning and sandy beaches for his 'by the sea'. More likely dismal skies, pale, bad-tempered people shivering on the rocky shore.

'Your father works in Peterhead?'

'Aye, he does.'

She had grown up listening to the proper English of the BBC World Service only to come to Britain and find people saying 'yes' like it was said back home in Arabic: 'aye'.

'What does he do, your father?'

He looked surprised, his blue eyes surprised, 'Ma dad's a joiner.'

Fareed hired people like that to work on the house. Ordered them about.

'And your mother?' she asked.

He paused a little, stirred sugar in his coffee with a plastic spoon. 'She's a lollipop lady.'

Shadia smirked into her coffee, took a sip.

'My father,' she said proudly, 'is a doctor, a specialist.' Her father was a gynaecologist. The woman who was now his wife had been one of his patients. Before that, Shadia's friends had teased her about her father's job, crude jokes that made her laugh. It was all so sordid now.

'And my mother,' she blew the truth up out of proportion,

'comes from a very big family. A ruling family. If you British hadn't colonized us, my mother would have been a princess now.'

'Ye walk like a princess,' he said.

What a gullible, silly boy! She wiped her forehead with her hand and said, 'You mean I am conceited and proud?'

'No, Ah didnae mean that, no . . .' The packet of sugar he was tearing open tipped from his hand, its contents scattered over the table. 'Ah shit . . . sorry . . .' He tried to scoop up the sugar and knocked against his coffee mug, spilling a little on the table.

She took out a tissue from her bag, reached over and mopped up the stain. It was easy to pick up all the bits of sugar with the damp tissue.

'Thanks,' he mumbled and they were silent. The cafeteria was busy; full of the humming, buzzing sound of people talking to each other, trays and dishes. In Khartoum, she avoided being alone with Fareed. She preferred it when they were with others: their families, their many mutual friends. If they were ever alone, she imagined that her mother or her sister was with them, could hear them, and she spoke to Fareed with that audience in mind.

Bryan was speaking to her, saying something about rowing on the River Dee. He went rowing on the weekends, he belonged to a rowing club.

To make herself pleasing to people was a skill Shadia was trained in. It was not difficult to please people. Agree with them, never dominate the conversation, be economical with the truth. Now, here was someone to whom all these rules needn't apply.

She said to him, 'The Nile is superior to the Dee. I saw your Dee, it is nothing, it is like a stream. There are two Niles, the Blue and the White, named after their colours. They come from

81

the south, from two different places. They travel for miles over countries with different names, never knowing they will meet. I think they get tired of running alone, it is such a long way to the sea. They want to reach the sea so that they can rest, stop running. There is a bridge in Khartoum, and under this bridge the two Niles meet. If you stand on the bridge and look down you can see the two waters mixing together.'

'Do ye get homesick?' he asked. She felt tired now, all this talk of the river running to rest in the sea. She had never talked like this before. Luxury words, and this question he asked.

'Things I should miss I don't miss. Instead I miss things I didn't think I would miss. The *azan*, the Muslim call to prayer from the mosque. I don't know if you know about it. I miss that. At dawn it used to wake me up. I would hear "prayer is better than sleep" and just go back to sleep. I never got up to pray.' She looked down at her hands on the table. There was no relief in confessions, only his smile, young, and something like wonder in his eyes.

'We did Islam in school,' he said. 'Ah went on a trip to Mecca.' He opened out his palms on the table.

'What!'

'In a book.'

'Oh.'

The coffee was finished. They should go now. She should go to the library before the next lecture and photocopy previous exam papers. Asafa, full of helpful advice, had shown her where to find them.

'What is your religion?' she asked.

'Dunno, nothing I suppose.'

'That's terrible! That's really terrible!' Her voice was too loud, concerned.

His face went red again and he tapped his spoon against the empty mug.

Waive all politeness, make him dislike her. Badr had said, even before his windows got smashed, that here in the West they hate Islam. Standing up to go, she said flippantly, 'Why don't you become a Muslim then?'

He shrugged, 'Ah wouldnae mind travelling to Mecca, I was keen on that book.'

Her eyes filled with tears. They blurred his face when he stood up. In the West they hate Islam and he ... She said, 'Thanks for the coffee,' and walked away, but he followed her.

'Shadiya, Shadiya,' he pronounced her name wrongly, three syllables instead of two, 'there's this museum about Africa. I've never been before. If you'd care to go, tomorrow ...'

◆

No sleep for the guilty, no rest, she should have said no, I can't go, no I have too much catching up to do. No sleep for the guilty, the memories come from another continent. Her father's new wife, happier than her mother, fewer worries. When Shadia visits she offers fruit in a glass bowl, icy oranges and guavas, soothing in the heat. Shadia's father hadn't wanted a divorce, hadn't wanted to leave them, he wanted two wives not a divorce. But her mother had too much pride, she came from fading money, a family with a 'name'. Of the new wife her mother says, bitch, whore, the dregs of the earth, a nobody.

Tomorrow she need not show up at the museum, even though she said that she would. She should have told Bryan she was engaged to be married, mentioned it casually. What did he expect from her? Europeans had different rules, reduced, abrupt customs. If Fareed knew about this ... her secret thoughts like snakes ... Perhaps she was like her father, a traitor. Her mother said that her father was devious. Sometimes Shadia was devious. With Fareed in the car, she would deliberately say, 'I need to stop at the grocer, we need things at home.' At the grocer he would pay for all her shopping and she would say, 'No, you shouldn't do that, no, you are too generous, you are embarrassing me.' With the money she saved, she would buy a blouse for her mother, nail varnish for her mother, a magazine, imported apples.

◆

It was strange to leave her desk, lock her room and go out on a Saturday. In the hall the telephone rang. It was Fareed. If he knew where she was going now . . . Guilt was like a hardboiled egg stuck in her chest. A large cold egg.

'Shadia, I want you to buy some of the fixtures for the bathrooms. Taps and towel hangers. I'm going to send you a list of what I want exactly and the money . . .'

'I can't, I can't.'

'What do you mean you can't? If you go into any large department store . . .'

'I can't, I wouldn't know where to put these things, how to send them.'

There was a rustle on the line and she could hear someone whispering, Fareed distracted a little. He would be at work this time in the day, glass bottles filling up with clear effervescent, the words 7Up written in English and Arabic, white against the dark green.

'You can get good things, things that aren't available here. Gold would be good. It would match . . .'

Gold. Gold toilet seats!

'People are going to burn in hell for eating out of gold dishes, you want to sit on gold!'

He laughed. He was used to getting his own way, not easily threatened, 'Are you joking with me?'

'No.'

In a quieter voice, 'This call is costing . . .'

She knew, she knew. He shouldn't have let her go away. She was not coping with the whole thing, she was not handling the stress. Like the Nigerian student.

'Shadia, gold-coloured, not gold. It's smart.'

'Allah is going to punish us for this, it's not right . . .'

'Since when have you become so religious!'

◆

Bryan was waiting for her on the steps of the museum, familiar-looking against the strange grey of the city streets where cars had their headlamps on in the middle of the afternoon. He wore a different shirt, a navy-blue jacket. He said, not looking at her, 'Ah was beginning to think you wouldnae turn up.'

There was no entry fee to the museum, no attendant handing out tickets. Bryan and Shadia walked on soft carpets; thick blue carpets that made Shadia want to take off her shoes. The first thing they saw was a Scottish man from Victorian times. He sat on a chair surrounded by possessions from Africa: overflowing trunks, an ancient map strewn on the floor of the glass cabinet. All the light in the room came from this and other glass cabinets and gleamed on the waxed floors. Shadia turned away; there was an ugliness in the life-like wispiness of his hair, his determined expression, the way he sat. A hero who had gone away and come back, laden, ready to report.

Bryan began to conscientiously study every display cabinet, to read the posters on the wall. She followed him around and thought that he was studious, careful; that was why he did so well in his degree. She watched the intent expression on his face as he looked at everything. For her the posters were an effort to read, the information difficult to take in. It had been so long since she had read anything outside the requirements of the course. But she persevered, saying the words to herself, moving her lips . . . *'During the 18th and 19th centuries, northeast Scotland made a disproportionate impact on the world at large by contributing so many skilled and committed individuals. In serving an empire they gave and received, changed others and were themselves changed and often returned home with tangible reminders of their experiences.'*

The tangible reminders were there to see, preserved in spite of the years. Her eyes skimmed over the disconnected objects out of place and time. Iron and copper, little statues. Nothing was of her, nothing belonged to her life at home, what she missed. Here was Europe's vision, the clichés about Africa; cold and old.

She had not expected the dim light and the hushed silence. Apart from Shadia and Bryan, there was only a man with a briefcase, a lady who took down notes, unless there were others out of sight on the second floor. Something electrical, the heating or the lights, gave out a humming sound like that of an air-conditioner. It made Shadia feel as if they were in an aeroplane without windows, detached from the world outside.

'He looks like you, don't you think?' she said to Bryan. They stood in front of a portrait of a soldier who died in the first year of the twentieth century. It was the colour of his eyes and his hair. But Bryan did not answer her, did not agree with her. He was preoccupied with reading the caption. When she looked at the portrait again, she saw that she was mistaken. That strength in the eyes, the purpose, was something Bryan didn't have. They had strong faith in those days long ago.

Biographies of explorers who were educated in Edinburgh; they knew what to take to Africa: doctors, courage, Christianity, commerce, civilization. They knew what they wanted to bring back: cotton – watered by the Blue Nile, the Zambezi River. She walked after Bryan, felt his concentration, his interest in what was before him and thought, 'In a photograph we would not look nice together.'

She touched the glass of a cabinet showing papyrus rolls, copper pots. She pressed her forehead and nose against the cool glass. If she could enter the cabinet, she would not make a good exhibit. She wasn't right, she was too modern, too full of mathematics.

Only the carpet, its petroleum blue, pleased her. She had come to this museum expecting sunlight and photographs of the Nile, something to relieve her homesickness: a comfort, a message. But the messages were not for her, not for anyone like her. A letter from West Africa, 1762, an employee to his employer in Scotland. An employee trading European goods for African curiosities. *It was difficult to make the natives understand my meaning, even by an interpreter, it being a thing so seldom asked of them, but they have all undertaken to bring something and laughed heartily at me and said, I was a good man to love their country so much ...*

Love my country so much. She should not be here, there was nothing for her here. She wanted to see minarets, boats fragile on the Nile, people. People like her father. The times she had sat in the waiting room of his clinic, among pregnant women, a pain in her heart because she was going to see him in a few minutes. His room, the air-conditioner and the smell of his pipe, his white coat. When she hugged him, he smelled of Listerine mouthwash. He could never remember how old she was, what she was studying; six daughters, how could he keep track. In his confusion, there was freedom for her, games to play, a lot of teasing. She visited his clinic in secret, telling lies to her mother. She loved him more than she loved her mother.

Her mother who did everything for her, tidied her room, sewed her clothes from *Burda* magazine. Shadia was twenty-five and her mother washed everything for her by hand, even her pants and bras.

'I know why they went away,' said Bryan, 'I understand why they travelled.' At last he was talking. She had not seen him intense before. He spoke in a low voice. 'They had to get away, to leave here . . .'

'To escape from the horrible weather . . .' she was making fun of him. She wanted to put him down. The imperialists who had humiliated her history were heroes in his eyes.

He looked at her. 'To escape . . .' he repeated.

'They went to benefit themselves,' she said, 'people go away because they benefit in some way.'

'I want to get away,' he said.

She remembered when he had opened his palms on the table and said, 'I went on a trip to Mecca.' There had been pride in his voice.

'I should have gone somewhere else for the course,' he went on. 'A new place, somewhere down south.'

He was on a plateau, not like her. She was fighting and struggling for a piece of paper that would say she was awarded an M.Sc. from a British university. For him, the course was a continuation.

'Come and see,' he said, and he held her arm. No one had touched her before, not since she had hugged her mother goodbye. Months now in this country and no one had touched her.

She pulled her arm away. She walked away, quickly up the stairs. Metal steps rattled under her feet. She ran up the stairs to the next floor. Guns, a row of guns aiming at her. They had been waiting to blow her away. Scottish arms of centuries ago, gunfire in service of the empire.

Silver muzzles, a dirty grey now. They must have shone prettily once, under a sun far away. If they blew her away now, where would she fly and fall? A window that looked out at the hostile sky. She shivered in spite of the wool she was wearing, layers of clothes. Hell is not only blazing fire, a part of it is freezing cold, torturous ice and snow. In Scotland's winter you have a glimpse of this unseen world, feel the breath of it in your bones.

There was a bench and she sat down. There was no one here on this floor. She was alone with sketches of jungle animals, words on the wall. A diplomat away from home, in Ethiopia in 1903; Asafa's country long before Asafa was born. *It is difficult to imagine anything more satisfactory or better worth taking part in than a lion drive. We rode back to camp feeling very well indeed. Archie was quite right when he said that this was the first time since we have started that we have really been in Africa – the real Africa of jungle inhabited only by game, and plains where herds of antelope meet your eye in every direction.*

'Shadiya, don't cry.' He still pronounced her name wrongly because she had not told him how to say it properly.

He sat next to her on the bench, the blur of his navy jacket blocking the guns, the wall-length pattern of antelope herds. She should explain that she cried easily, there was no need for the alarm on his face. His awkward voice: 'Why are ye crying?'

He didn't know, he didn't understand. He was all wrong, not a substitute . . .

'They are telling lies in this museum,' she said. 'Don't believe them. It's all wrong. It's not jungles and antelopes, it's people. We have things like computers and cars. We have 7Up in Africa, and some people, a few people, have bathrooms with golden taps . . . I shouldn't be here with you. You shouldn't talk to me . . .'

He said, 'Museums change, I can change . . .'

He didn't know it was a steep path she had no strength for. He didn't understand. Many things, years and landscapes, gulfs. If she had been strong she would have explained, and not tired of explaining. She would have patiently taught him another language, letters curved like the epsilon and gamma he knew from mathematics. She would have shown him that words could be read from right to left. If she not been small in the museum, if she had been really strong, she would have made his trip to Mecca real, not only in a book.

IFEOMA OKOYE

The Power of a Plate of Rice

I walked hurriedly to Mr Aziza's office, breathing heavily in steadily rising anger. The January sun was blazing in fury, taking undue advantage of the temporary withdrawal of the seasonal harmattan. As I arrived at the office which was at the end of the administration block, I remembered one of my mother's precepts: 'Do nothing in anger. Wait till your anger melts like thick palm oil placed under the sun.' Mother was a philosopher of sorts. Poor woman. She died before I could reward her for all the sacrifices she made on my behalf, forgoing many comforts just so that I could get some education, and for carrying the financial burden of the family during my father's protracted illness and even after his premature death. In deference to Mother, I stood by Mr Aziza's door for a few seconds, trying to stifle my anger, but failing woefully. Only an angel or an idiot would remain calm in my situation.

At last I knocked at the mottled green door.

'Come in.'

Mr Aziza's authoritative voice hit me like a blow, startling me. I opened the door and walked in, my anger still smouldering . . .

Mr Aziza, the principal of the secondary school where I was teaching, was seated behind a medium-sized desk made of cheap white wood and thickly coated with varnish. Books, files, letter trays and loose sheets of paper jostled for a place on the desk. He raised his coconut-shaped head, closed the file he was reading, removed his plastic-framed spectacles and peered at me.

'Yes, Mrs Cheta Adu. What do you want?' His voice was on the defensive and the look on his ridged face was intimidating.

I took a deep breath. 'The bursar has just told me, Sir, that you told him to withhold my salary.'

We were paid irregularly. Although it was the end of January, the salary in question was for October of the previous year. Four months without any salary and yet we went to work regularly.

'Yes, I did, Mrs Cheta Adu.' Mr Aziza's small, narrow eyes pierced me like a lethal weapon. As one teacher had put it, he paralysed his prey with his eyes before dealing a death blow to them.

'What have I done, Sir?' I asked, trying to load the word *Sir* with as much sarcasm as I could to indicate how I felt inside.

Mr Aziza fingered his bulbous nose, a part of his body which had been the butt of many a teacher's joke. He was known to love food more than anything else, and one female teacher had once said that most of what he ate went into his nose.

'You were away from school without permission for four days last week,' Mr Aziza finally declared.

My anger, which a few minutes ago had reduced to a simmer, suddenly began to bubble like a pot of *ogbono* soup when the fire under it is poked.

I said as calmly as I could, 'In those four days, Sir, I almost lost my baby. I had already explained the circumstances to you. My baby became very ill suddenly. I had to rush him to hospital. For those four days, Sir, he battled for his life.'

'And so?' Mr Aziza intoned.

Someone knocked at the door and I turned to see the Second Vice-Principal's bearded face appear as he opened it. 'I'll be back,' a thin-lipped, hair-fringed mouth said and disappeared. The appearance of the bearded face was like a comic scene in a Shakespearean tragedy.

I turned to Mr Aziza and, in answer to his question, I reminded him that I had sent someone to tell him that my baby was in hospital.

'After you've been away from school for days,' Mr Aziza complained.

'Yes, Sir, but my baby was in real danger and I was too upset to write. I had thought you would understand.'

'And did you bother to find out whether your friend gave your message to me or not?'

'She told me she delivered it a day after I sent her to you. You were not in the office when she first called, and then she forgot all about it till the next day. I've already apologized for all the delay, Sir.'

Mr Aziza opened another file and began to flip through it. 'You will receive your salary at the end of February,' he said.

I gasped, 'Do you mean I'll have to wait till the end of February before I receive my salary?'

'Exactly.'

'That would make it five whole months without a salary!'

'I'm not interested in your calculations.'

Mr Aziza was known for punishing his teachers by withholding their salaries. But I had not known him to withhold any teacher's salary for more than two weeks at the most. He had always felt, and had said so in words and in action, that he was doing his teachers a favour by paying them even though the school belonged to, and was funded by, the state government.

'How am I going to feed my two sons, Sir?' I asked.

'That's your problem, not mine,' Mr Aziza replied.

I refused to think about this problem. January, as every low- and medium-salaried worker in my country knows from experience, was the longest month of the year. After the enormous compulsive and often senseless spending during

Christmas and the New Year, a salaried worker was left with little money for the rest of January. And for those who had children in school, paying school fees and buying books and school uniforms for the new school year often became a nightmare. This year was worse for me because I and all the other teachers in the school were last paid in September of the year before.

'I am a widow, Sir,' I pleaded with Mr Aziza. 'I am the sole bread-winner for my family. Times are hard. My children cannot survive till the end of February without my next salary.'

Mr Aziza said, 'I don't want to know, Mrs Cheta Adu. My decision is final.'

He stood up, hitched his trousers up with his elbows, and walked to a window on his right and peered out of it. He was a small, wiry man, the type my mother often told me to beware of.

Helpless, I stood watching him, a man known for his inflexibility. I knew from my colleagues' experiences that taking my case to the State Schools Management Board would be futile as Mr Aziza had ingratiated himself with the powerful and high-ranking officers of the Board. As the principal of one of the elite schools in the state, he had helped them to get their children admitted into his school even when the spoilt ones amongst them did not pass the entrance examination. I also knew that taking Mr Aziza to court was out of the question. Where would I get the money for a lawyer? Besides, civil cases had been known to last for months or even years because of unnecessary and often deliberate court adjournments.

Mr Aziza walked back to his chair and sat down.

I looked hard at him and, without saying anything more, left his office. In a taxi taking me home, I thought about nothing else but Mr Aziza. This was the second time I had found myself at his mercy. The first time was when, five years before, I was transferred to his school from a secondary school in Onitsha where I was teaching before my marriage. On reading the letter posting me to his school – I had delivered it to him personally – he had flung it at me and had declared, 'I don't want any more female teachers in my school, especially married ones.'

'What have we done?' I had wanted to know.

'You're a lazy lot,' he had said. 'You always find excuses to be away from school. Today it's this child of yours becoming ill who must be taken to hospital, and tomorrow it's the funeral of one relation or another.'

When he officially refused to give me a place in his school, I resorted to a tactic I had used successfully before. I kept calling at his office every day, often without uttering a word, until I broke his resistance and made him accept me. This time, however, I had the feeling that he would not budge, no matter what I did.

When I arrived home after five in the evening, my mother-in-law was walking up and down in front of my flat with my two-year-old son, Rapulu, tied on her back, and four-year-old Dulue trailing behind her.

'You're late, Cheta,' my mother-in-law said. 'I was beginning to think you were not going to come home.' She looked weary and worried.

'Sorry, Mama, I have some problems at school.' I walked to her after hugging Dulue, who had trotted to me. 'And how is Rap?' I asked.

'He's ill.'

I placed the back of my hand on my younger son's forehead. It was piping hot.

'You're not going to be ill again, Rapulu?' I said under my breath. Aloud I asked, 'How long has he been running a temperature, Mama?'

'A short while after you left for school in the morning,' my mother-in-law replied.

I helped her untie Rapulu from her back and took him in, Dulue trotting behind me. I stripped Rapulu of his clothes, put him on the settee, fetched a bowl of cold water and a towel and began to sponge him down. He yelled and kicked, but I ignored him. Dulue, with his thumb in his mouth, kept on mumbling that he was hungry, while my mother-in-law stood speechless, watching me.

Presently, I remembered that I should have given Rapulu some fever medicine. I ran into the only bedroom in the flat and dashed out with a small bottle. Taking Rapulu in my arms, I gave him a teaspoonful of the bitter-sweet medicine and began to sponge him again.

My mother-in-law soon dozed off. Poor woman, she must have had a trying day. She was a widow too and I had brought her to help me look after my children. Bless her, for what could I have done if she had refused my offer? Another reason why I brought her to live with me was to save costs. I used to send her money every month to supplement the meagre proceeds from her farms.

We had a late lunch of yam and raw palm oil. It was the last piece of yam in the house. I skipped supper because I wanted to make sure that the *garri* and *egusi* soup which I had left would last for two nights.

The night was a long one. First I lay awake for fear that Rapulu might become worse, but fortunately the fever did not persist. Then I reviewed all that I had gone through since I lost Afam, my husband who was an only child, in a ghastly motor accident a little more than a year before. He was a brilliant banker. We were at the university together, he studying banking and I mathematics. As luck would have it, we were posted to the same state for our National Youth Service. We became engaged at the end of our service and married shortly after. He died a fortnight after our fifth wedding anniversary and, ever since, my life had become an endless journey into the land of hardship and frustration. I had, under great pressure, spent all our savings to give my husband what my people and his had called a befitting burial, and what I saw as a senseless waste of hard-earned money.

For the better part of the night, I worried over how I was going to pay the January rent, how I was going to feed my two sons and my mother-in-law, and what I was going to do if Rapulu became so ill that he had to be hospitalized again. I already owed two of my friends some money and could not see myself summoning up the courage to go to them again.

I borrowed money again and for two long weeks I managed to feed my family, sometimes going without meals myself. I became irritable, and students complained that I was being too hard on them. My good natured mother-in-law became equally touchy and nagged me incessantly. My two sons threw tantrums, spending a great deal of time crying. Soon I had no money left and no one to lend me more. I had reached a point when I had to do something drastic or allow my sons to die of hunger.

On the 23rd of February, after school hours, I went to Mr Aziza's office and once again pleaded with him to pay me.

'You're wasting your time, Mrs Cheta Adu,' he said. 'I never change my mind. You will receive your salary on the twenty-eighth of February and not even one day earlier.'

I left his office and waited for him in the outer room. At four o'clock he left his office. I followed him to his house, which was situated near the school main gate, and he turned and asked me why I was following him. I remained silent. He opened the door and walked in. Quietly, I followed him into his sitting-room and sat down without any invitation to do so. The room was sparsely furnished. A black-and-white television stood on top of the shelf next to a small transistor radio. Near the bookshelf was a small dining table and a steel-back chair.

Mr Aziza lived alone. His wife and six children lived at Onitsha about one hundred and twenty kilometres away.

Mr Aziza turned and faced me. 'Look, Mrs Adu, you'll achieve nothing by following me like a dog. You may stay here forever, but you'll not make me change my mind.' He disappeared through a door on the right.

Presently, his houseboy walked into the room and began to lay the table. The smell of *jollof* rice wafted around my nostrils, reactivating in me the hunger which had been suppressed by anger, depression, and desperation. The houseboy finished laying the table and left.

On impulse I left my chair, walked to the dining table and sat down on the chair beside it. Removing the lid on the plate, I stared at the appetizing mound of *jollof* rice. Then I grabbed the spoon beside the plate and began to eat. I ate quickly, and not only with relish, but also with vengeance and animosity.

I heard a door squeak and turned to see Mr Aziza walk into the sitting-room. His jaw dropped and his mouth remained open as he stared at me.

'What do you think you're doing, Mrs Cheta Adu?' he bellowed, finding his tongue at last. Disbelief was writen all over his face.

I ignored the question and continued to help myself to the rice. I scooped a large piece of meat and some rice into my mouth, my cheeks bulging.

Mr Aziza strode to the table, snatched the spoon from me with his right hand and with his left snatched the plate of rice away from me. It was almost empty by now. I rose from the chair and moved a little bit back from him, thinking he was going to hit me.

He faced me, his eyes deadly. 'Get out of my house, I say, get out!'

'Not until I receive my salary,' I said calmly. Desperation had given me a form of courage I had not experienced before. 'I'll wait for supper.'

Mr Aziza barked at me. 'Get out. Go to the bursar. Tell him I said he can pay you now.'

I said calmly, 'He'll not believe me. Why not give me a note for him?'

He scribbled a note, threw it at me and I grabbed it. Trying hard to suppress a smile, I said, 'Thank you, Sir,' and left the room, still chewing the rubbery meat in my mouth.

LILIA MOMPLE

Stress

The major-general's lover stares at the man sitting on the second-floor balcony and whispers, indignantly: 'Drunkard.'

She can see him clearly, leaning back in the worn leather chair, a transistor radio on a side table, a glass of beer in his hand. 'Drunkard,' she repeats, without taking her eyes off the man. 'He's going to drink all afternoon.'

The man is downing the beer with ill-contained voracity, his attention focused on the glass and radio. For a moment, a very brief moment, the major-general's lover thinks he is aware of her presence, but then realizes, as always, that his glancing look excludes her. It is entirely filled by the radio and glass of beer.

Sunday, and as happens every Sunday at this time, the major-general's lover goes on to the balcony overlooking the street. She has lunched alone in the vast living-room that might have been bright and airy, given its size, white walls and the large glass door opening on to the balcony. Yet it is a sombre place, owing to the profusion of furniture made of precious and very dark *jambire* wood, wall-to-wall carpeting, metal knick-knacks, velvet armchairs and heavy curtains. Even the dust seems agitated as it circulates in the room.

The living-room is indeed a place that arouses, in visitors with a sensitive spirit, a deep and insidious melancholy which, sometimes in mid-conversation, makes them hurriedly take their leave, as if suddenly unable to breathe in that luxury allied with flagrant bad taste. An urgency drives them out into the street.

100

However, for the major-general's lover this is her realm, replete with furniture, wall-to-wall carpeting, curtains, and with the knick-knacks she herself chose and the major-general bought without haggling over high prices and questionable utility. That is why she feels so well here; just as when a while ago when she was having lunch, seated at the huge *jambire* table, served by a silent and efficient servant, she felt her head swim with the intoxicating sensation caused by the fact that everything her eyes fell on belonged to her.

After lunch the relaxing ritual of dressing and making up merely increased her current good mood. It was a ritual to which she gave herself with all the zeal of women who live alone and seek, through their carefully groomed appearance, to compensate for solitude.

Already in the bedroom, she took off the robe she had been wearing since her morning bath, in which she so much liked to wander through the apartment on Sunday mornings. She then exchanged it for the dress she had chosen the day before. It was silk shantung – sea-green, clinging – with a generously cut-out neckline repeated at the back, buttoned down to the belt with tiny buttons. The modern note was given by the wide belt and the sleeves with lots of pleats at the shoulder, which ended just above the elbow. After putting on her dress and shoes, the major-general's lover looked at herself in the mirror with approval, aware how well the dress fitted her thin and sinuous body, and that the sea-green enhanced the amber of her light *mulata* skin.

She then put astringent on her face and waited for it to be fully absorbed. After that she put on base, with light and rapid pats, followed by judicious circular massaging, until her skin took on the luminous look that only quality products impart. It was then time to put on very fine scented powder, a touch of blusher on her cheeks, and to emphasize the contours of her lips with red ochre lipstick. Finally, making up her eyes required the greatest care to blend the eye-shadows on her lids, and to draw an impeccable stroke with eye-liner, close to the lashes, in turn lengthened with a little mascara.

Only then, after putting a last dab of perfume on her ear lobe, and looking again approvingly at the image thrown back by the mirror, did the major-general's lover feel ready to leave the bedroom.

Now, as on every Sunday afternoon since she has lived in the flat, she is waiting for her lover on the balcony overlooking the street, meanwhile offering herself to the eyes of passers-by and neighbours.

At this time the street is almost deserted and a dull tedium hangs in the air, latent during weekdays, and becoming almost palpable on Sunday afternoons.

Tedium is secreted by the blocks of flats and houses: uncharacteristic constructions of a wearisome beauty, designed in colonial times by Portuguese entrepreneurs with lots of money and dubious taste. Yet it might also be the inhabitants of the blocks of flats and houses who are the cause of the tedium.

Some already lived there in colonial times. These are mostly Portuguese who, though they did not leave the country after Independence, are still bitterly resentful of Mozambicans, and remember the time when no black would so much as dare pass down this street.

Others are foreign aid workers of all kinds – of European and American origin. They are hardly seen in the street, since they enter and leave their shiny cars and, on weekends, fly to South Africa or Swaziland, or else fill themselves with alcohol, in the company of other foreign-aid workers, in the city's tourist complexes and nightclubs. They are creatures who are very fearful of the 'thieving instincts' of Mozambicans, which is why they shelter behind metal grille walls, protected by fierce dogs and guards they keep on duty day and night.

Yet others are black, whole families come from the suburbs. They came immediately after the nationalization of apartment blocks, their heads filled with dreams and hopes as if the fact of coming to occupy these homes would automatically entitle them to lead the same lives of ease as the settlers who had abandoned them. However, reality proved very miserly, and today they live in poverty. They question their own deep-rooted principles passed on from generation to generation. They take in all the relatives who arrive from the bush in great numbers, having fled from the war, bringing only the ragged clothes that cover their maimed bodies – in their blank eyes the images of the horror that made them leave their land. The hostile city that does not need them, refuses their inept adaptation.

Finally, another type of people had come to live in the street. Payers of key money, people of all races for whom, as a rule, money was not hard to earn and who, in exchange for a few million, managed to make the real tenants leave their homes. Leases in changed names.

The major-general's lover was a payer of key money. She had spent all her life in a flat in Malhandalene, but as soon as she became the major-general's lover she started to complain that she could no longer stand that unfit place, with problems of water, rubbish, lack of security, bad neighbours, everything. Until one day, on one of his Sunday visits, the major-general, even before greeting her, said triumphantly: 'Come and see the place where you're going to live now.'

He had paid a good few million to buy the keys to the flat, in the middle of the Polana neighbourhood, from a civil servant couple who, squeezed by the constant rise in the cost of living, decided to return to their suburban Mafalala, and illegally transferred the lease to the name of the major-general's lover, who has been living here for more than two years.

Now, on the balcony, she looks down a long stretch of road which, as always, has nothing new to offer. The same children playing on the pavements, the same cars gliding silently by, their occupants very aware of the high esteem in which they hold themselves. The same *chapas*,[1] nearly empty because it's Sunday, but creaking painfully.

And also the visitors to the patients in the Central Hospital, at the very end of the street. They are usually people of modest means for whom such visits are a duty and a Sunday pastime. There goes a group now, a man a little ahead, squeezed into a threadbare old jacket, his face shining with sweat from the long walk from the suburbs, tripping from tiredness and his down-at-heel mud-spattered shoes. Following a little behind are three women, dragging their feet in plastic sandals. Two of them carry on their heads cooking pots wrapped in faded tablecloths and the other, a bit younger, looks exhausted from carrying one child on her back and another in her belly. From time to time they talk to each other, but soon stop in order to concentrate on walking, leaning forward like trees beaten by the wind.

The major-general's lover looks at all this in disgust. Were it not for the man sitting on the balcony opposite, she would already have returned to her soft velvet sofa to wait for the lover who should be coming soon. But something stronger than herself keeps her standing there, waging the silent and inglorious struggle that has been going on since the first Sunday when, after her solitary lunch, she dressed, made herself up, perfumed herself and went on to the balcony.

That first Sunday the man was there, sitting in the worn

[1] Minibus taxis.

104

leather chair, absorbed with the radio and the beer he was to go on drinking all afternoon. That serious and melancholy face immediately pleased her, despite his extremely young features. And also his hands, bony and nervous, which held the glass of beer with the firm delicacy of someone strumming the chords of an instrument.

The man, however, ignored the presence of the woman looking at him from her balcony, very available and convinced of her powers of seduction. And he continued to ignore her every Sunday for two years.

Had he even once shown any interest, the major-general's lover might immediately have forgotten him. Conversely, this way, and against her own will, she began to desire him with a fierceness alien to her cold and calculating nature, starting even to spy on him at the times when he came home and went out, hurrying and serious, with his briefcase under his arm. And so many times, on feeling the major-general's chubby hands pass over her body, she imagines how different the fingering of those other bony and nervous hands would be. And so many times, in the brief lapse of a kiss, she seeks in the worn face of her lover that other face, young, deeply touched with melancholy.

The major-general's lover is the first to acknowledge the senselessness of this desire for a virtually unknown man. All she knows about him is that he is a secondary school teacher, married with four children, and that his flat is packed with relatives who have fled from the war. She also calculates that, though educated, he is doubtless very poor. And she who all her life felt an instinctive repugnance for poor people, including her own family, starts to doll herself up every Sunday especially for a penniless teacher who doesn't even see her. And the most annoying part of it for the offended woman is the fact that she cannot find consolation in the covetous eyes of other men, because it is from this one that she demands confirmation of her femininity and beauty.

This is why now, radiant in her sea-green dress, on seeing him focused on the drink and radio, the major-general's lover continues to stare at him with a look of rancour. The same look he will see in the not too distant future, seated on the defendant's bench and, perplexed, ask himself: 'Why does that woman I hardly know hate me so much?'

That day, the major-general's lover will be the only witness for the prosecution. Not even his wife's relatives will testify against him because, despite being illiterate peasants, they bear within them ancient wisdom that enables them to distinguish between a criminal and a man driven by despair.

However, the major-general's lover, as soon as she learns of the tragedy, daring even to go against her lover, will put herself forward as witness for the prosecution, making the most of her privileged position as neighbour of the defendant. And at that hour of vengeance, she will incriminate the teacher with reckless and false statement. 'The defendant committed the crime with premeditation. I don't think he likes women!'

This statement will cause a wave of laughter among the spectators and make the judge order the witness to refrain from giving personal opinions. She will continue to stare at the defendant with triumph when, despite all the extenuating circumstances, a heavy sentence of fifteen years in prison is handed down.

On this tedious Sunday afternoon the major-general's lover continues to look at the teacher with the same malevolent glare, stopping only on the arrival of her lover, who has just got out of his Volvo. Then she runs into the flat. He likes to be met at the living-room door.

They greet one another without kisses or embraces. The

major-general, married for more than twenty years, adapts to a lover only in bed. There he melts into caresses with fierce impetuousness. When not in bed he prefers to assume the role of the friend and protector who is concerned about his friend's welfare, demanding only gratitude and respect.

The major-general is a man in his forties, short and nervous, who still retains the integrity of his time as a Frelimo guerrilla. That integrity remained noteworthy during the first years of Independence, gradually becoming more diluted as the 'civil war' dragged on, and he was promoted to ever higher posts.

Now, not only his integrity, but the ideas that had guided him during the Liberation Struggle, and for which he was prepared to sacrifice his very life, are also weakening, giving place to an unbridled desire to enjoy everything in life that gives him pleasure.

So it is not surprising that his belly, stuffed with good food and drink, is now large and flaccid, projecting from his body like a grotesque pregnancy. Or that his look should have acquired a dull coldness.

As always when he has just arrived, he walks around the living-room with his hands in his pockets, though there is little space to move in. Finally, he settles into one of the velvet armchairs, next to the marble-topped coffee table, where his lover puts out the glasses and the drinks she goes to get from a well-stocked cupboard.

She prepares a double whisky with ice for the major-general and a Campari for herself. Long ago she stopped trying to convince her lover to prepare and serve the drinks (according to worldly magazines, this is the man's job). He refuses to accept that norm of etiquette, which is 'just for faggots', as he says. Sitting facing one another, they drink slowly in small sips, as is proper when one has filled oneself with the best wines at lunch. They talk little, about trivial matters, but enjoy each other's company, especially because of their anticipation of the sin it includes.

The major-general's lover also finds it very flattering that he reserves Sunday afternoons and nights for her, for only on exceptional occasions does he spend them with his wife and children. So although she doesn't love him, she always treats him with attentive deference. She likes the prospect of dining out in a luxury restaurant, as has been their habit since they became lovers, and, later at night, of sharing her bed with a man.

Now, sipping her Campari and talking about pleasant things (not war or other boring matters), she is almost able to free herself from her obsession with the man who is still sitting on the balcony opposite, who ignores and humiliates her every Sunday.

Meanwhile, the teacher, unaware of the distress and rage he is provoking, listens attentively to the football commentary while drinking the beer which, in its bitter aftertaste, today contains a tinge of remorse. Remorse has been with him since morning, when his wife saw him arriving with the two half-litre bottles he had gone to buy at the corner shop.

'Don't forget the books and clothes for the children. One of these days they'll start to get bad marks for discipline,' she said, deliberately staring at the bottles of beer.

'All right. I'll deal with it tomorrow,' the teacher retorted, hurriedly putting the bottles into the empty fridge.

It is not so much his wife's implicit criticism that annoys him, but the fact that he was forced to lie to appease her. He is well aware that there will be no money tomorrow to buy school books and clothes for the children, and that probably he will barely be able to feed them. Hence the taste of remorse in the beer the teacher is drinking slowly, so as to make it last until the end of the commentary. Yet he is also aware that without these few hours of evasion on Sundays, a kind of ritual of which the football and drink are a part, he won't be able to stand the monotonous passing of his days.

He always wakes up feeling that he is already late, dresses in a rush and hurriedly drinks a cup of near-bitter tea (sugar is expensive) and eats a slice of dry bread. He always feels a strong desire for coffee, which he likes very much, but he cannot afford that luxury. He then runs to the secondary school where he teaches. He goes on foot, because there are no buses in the city and the price of *chapas* is prohibitive for him. He arrives at school sweating and aware that most of his energy has been spent before starting work.

He has always liked teaching and is one of the few teachers at the school who took up a teaching career as a calling. Yet all his initial enthusiasm has been wasting away in the face of classes of fifty pupils packed into classrooms, with minimum conditions for absorbing the lessons. Most of them are adolescents who despise both studying and the teachers themselves, especially those, like him, who don't accept bribes. And who, for that reason, present themselves in threadbare clothes, with down-at-heel and even torn shoes, appearing every day out of breath and sweating because they don't have their own cars or money for *chapas*.

When classes end at about one o'clock, the teacher rushes home, where a meagre meal awaits him and provides barely enough strength to correct exercises and then go to teach at night school. Finally, at around midnight, he returns home, exhausted and bitter, and falls into bed like a drunkard, only to wake up next morning with the eternal feeling that he is already late. And the race starts again, from morning till night.

Ah! Recently there have been a few surprises. They were the relatives who had fled from the war and knew they could find shelter in the home of the teacher, since he had drunk with his mother's milk the sense of hospitality that led him to receive them and share with them the little he had.

The latest fugitive was an aunt who, being a widow without children, had lived in Manhica, an area intensely affected by war, with her father, the teacher's maternal grandfather. The old man must have been over eighty and had always refused to leave his hut and the place where his dead were buried. Indeed, it might have been said that the dead protected him from the other world, because in the frequent attacks by Renamo in that area, he was always spared, even causing some suspicion among the population that he had an understanding with the *matchangas*.[2]

One day, however, when he was sitting at the hut door, his legs stretched out to warm them in the sun, a group of *matchangas* suddenly appeared, armed with rifles and machetes. One of them, probably the leader, ordered: 'Old man, give us something to eat!'

The grandfather, who had been slumbering, woke up still absorbed in his dreams, and looked at the men, smiling at them with his toothless mouth.

'Old man, give us something to eat!' the one who seemed to be the leader again demanded.

The grandfather's dim eyes could barely make out the newcomers, let alone their cruel scowls, rifles and machetes. Nor did his ears catch the gruff and urgent words. So he just sat there, still smiling, even when the man who did the talking snarled angrily: 'This old man is annoying me!' Then, taking a much used machete, he cut off his head. The head fell straight as a trophy, the eyes glassy and the mouth wide open, next to the body that remained leaning against the hut, slowly becoming soaked in blood.

[2] Insurgents – named after André Matchangaissa, founder of Renamo.

110

SINDIWE MAGONA

A State of Outrage

! How? Hawu! How? Hawu! How?
! How? Hawu! How? Hawu! How? . . .

er Mngomeni's voice boomed into the eerie
packed church hall.

ed the thick fog in Nana's mind. But that
uell the ball of worms in the pit of her
vent on writhing . . . writhing . . . churning
th came in long, slow, deliberate gasps. Her
y limp on her knees: one open flat, palm
loosely fisted. Her large eyes stared out,
were glassy and vacant. Thick, warm, slug-
wn the walls of her mouth, formed a pool
, oozed through, seeped up and slowly
by bit, her tongue was covered. Bit by bit,
nouth was completely dammed. And the

;ag if she swallowed the castor oil-like liquid.
ht the fisted hand to her mouth, put it there
ie surprised. She spewed the mass into the
andkerchief buried against the palm. Lethar-
dabbed at the corners of the mouth before
esting place. However, whatever relief it had
nort-lived. Up and down went her shoulders.
nthinkingly. Long, slow, shallow intakes of
the heaving mass, the rebellion, in her
Iot shots of pain flashed. Stay down! Hand

114

The teacher's aunt saw all this through a crack in the small wooden window of her room. All this she saw, trembling with fear and indignation, without being able to help her old father or even cry out.

The *matchangas* finally entered the hut, and she had just enough time to escape into the yard and run to a hiding place in the bush, where she stayed until they had gone. When she returned to the hut she found it completely sacked. And, like a lugubrious sentinel, her old father was there, his body stiff and bloody, his head beside him, his mouth open, smiling for eternity.

Moaning in her distress, the teacher's aunt buried the old man with her own hands, under the cashew tree where the family dead lay. After the solitary ceremony, she did not rest for a moment and, driven by sorrow and fear, walked without stopping and without distinguishing day from night, until she arrived in Maputo where, after countless vicissitudes and much despair, she finally found her nephew. He of course welcomed her, though his flat was already overcrowded with his and his wife's relatives, and his aunt was another mouth to feed and another body to provide shelter for.

The teacher's life, therefore, was not so much a life but a continual struggle to provide sustenance for the family, while maintaining basic dignity. For this reason, listening to the football commentary and drinking beer, on Sunday afternoons, was for him the only oasis.

There had been a time when some colleagues had brought beer and joined him to hear the football commentary. But beer had become increasingly expensive and, one by one, his colleagues had decided to meet in the house of a clandestine seller of *tontono*,[3] where they could enjoy themselves for less money.

[3] An illegal distilled drink.

111

Unfortunately, the teacher couldn't stand even the smell of *tontono*, so he ended up alone with his beer, now reduced to two half-litre bottles.

His wife had always understood his need for evasion on Sunday afternoons. Yet, as the privations became more acute, her understanding also decreased. And that morning, for the first time, she had criticized him, looking at the beer bottles he had hastily put in the fridge. And now, also for the first time, taking advantage of the absence of the family, who felt obliged to go for a walk on a Sunday afternoon, his wife invades his sacred space and, planting herself in front of him, demands books and clothes for the children and even clothes for herself, which is understandable, since she has only two faded dresses.

'But not here, please, not now,' he beseeches, though he remains silent, trying to hear the commentary amid his wife's demands. 'A long pass by Chiquinho . . .'

'The shoes are completely worn out . . .'

'A boundary kick by . . .'

'One day they'll fail because they don't have materials . . .'

'Goal, goal, goal by . . .'

'I really feel ashamed to go out in the street . . .'

'Advance, pass the ball and give the goal to . . .'

He can no longer hear the commentary because his wife, whose patience seems to have reached breaking point, has gone into a state of frenzy and is shouting loudly, completely drowning out the voice of the commentator.

Slowly, very slowly, like someone moving in another dimension, the teacher rises from the chair and, going towards his wife, who looks at him perplexed, puts both his hands around her throat and squeezes, squeezes, until she stops struggling and finally slides down and falls inert on the floor.

Her husband leaves her there and goes back to the leather-covered chair, listening to the commentary to the end and

drinking the beer to t
see his wife, lying on t
sees his own amazeme
expression of the fac
from the floor and ca
where he lays her, with

A little later, at the p
duty and confesses, in
I killed my wife.'

'You killed your wi
since he is unable to
murder.

'Yes, I killed her,' the
'Why? What was the
persists in a tone more
'I don't know. I just k
'You don't know? Yo
'I don't know. I am
teacher.

brushed tummy down. Then, please, Lord, don't let me get sick. Please, not here. Not now.

Hawu! How? Hawu! How? Hawu! How? . . .

Disbelief and bewilderment married in her mind. The din would not abate. Would not go away. She still could not believe what had brought her . . . brought everyone there . . . to that place. That day. Unreal.

From a distance, an organ sounded. There was singing too.

Njengebhadi Libhadula,
Ukufun' umthombo[1]

Reflex, almost. Or, in a dream. She stood up and sat down. Wide open were her eyes. Unseeing. She'd somehow got separated from her group and found herself sandwiched between an old woman with a mean alto on one side and another about her own age on the other. The veined hands of the alto thrust a hymn book under her nose. Nana completely ignored this. No point. She had lost her voice. Couldn't sing. Could not sing. Not here. Not today. Couldn't believe it. Although, of course, deep in some remote recess of her mind, she knew it was all real. Horribly real. Too true.

Who had picked her up from the airport, last night?

Herman Mba. Who was with him in the car? Sidney Siko. Lindiwe Mgcina. Sipho Kente. All former classmates. More. They were known as the Significant Six. Top of their class. Top Six. Way back then.

Droning on, the priest came to the front of the pulpit and sprinkled something all over the oblong box. Long. Sleek. Silent. The action pulled Nana's eyes, forced them to focus,

---

[1] *As the hart wanders,*
In search of a stream.

follow his movements. Look. Witness. A shudder splintered her spine. Now there are five, she thought, casting an accusing look at the coffin. Oh, Wayidyuduza! Hot pain seared across the bottom of her stomach as though she had taken a knife with her own hand, plunged it in at one side, drawn it across – from left to right. Slowly. Deeply. That tangible the pain. She gasped.

'Are you okay?' her other neighbour, the younger woman, asked.

Head bent, Nana nodded. Her eyes were smarting.

'Why don't you sit down?'

Ffwiisshh! With a swish and a rustle, she flopped onto the seat. She felt her legs tremble beneath her. Small tremors tore from ankle, through calf, to knee. Staring straight ahead, she stretched her legs in front of her, as far as the back of the seat to the front of her would allow. Opened her eyes wide. She wouldn't cry. No, she would not cry.

'Did you know her? Are you a relative?' The young woman bent down to whisper her concern.

Again, Nana's head went up and down. Once. The motion was barely perceptible.

How old had they been? Ten? Eleven? The year Vuyokazi Rhadebe came to their school, Entseni Primary. Her family had moved from somewhere in the Orange Free State to Cape Town. An odd time of the school year it was too, she remembered. Not January or June, the usual times for the arrival of new students. As the only newcomer, Vuyokazi should have been endlessly teased. But she had suffered hardly any initiation at all. Her undisguised aversion to pain, and her picture-book good looks, quickly earned her support from the older pupils, thus shielding her from the bullies. Her outgoing, bubbly personality, together with a certain air of tragedy she possessed, ensured that none of the other students harboured

116

resentment against her. Not for long, at any rate. Which was just as well, for she got into scraps quite often. Full of mischief, she was. A prankster. But when anyone confronted her, all she needed to do was to turn those little-girl-lost, luminous eyes on that person and sniff, brows arched slightly, one hand scratching furiously at the back of her head. At this sight of her everyone was immediately reminded that she had recently lost a brother and a sister in a fire, and that she was now an only child.

Tall and far from scrawny, she looked quite the athlete. With great enthusiasm and lofty expectations, the teachers tried the newcomer out. One sport after the other: netball; softball; the three-legged race; high jump; long jump; the one-hundred-yards race and other track events. Hopeless, hopeless, hopeless. A *klutz*. Charming. Vivacious. But she could never catch a ball, or throw it where it was supposed to go. She couldn't run to save her own skin. Even when given the longest lead in the relay race, if Vuyokazi didn't lose the lead, she'd drop the stick or in some other manner cause her side to lose the game anyway.

'Oh Wayidyuduza! Look what you've done,' Mrs Mabuya, who supervised the girls' sports, cried out one day in exasperation. And the name stuck. For the rest of the time, three years, she attended Entseni, everyone, including the teachers, called her Wayidyuduza. Why, she even called herself by that name.

After primary school, they went to different high schools. Some even went away to boarding schools in the Ciskei and the Transkei. Wayidyuduza went to a boarding school in the Transkei. Bensonvale? Yes, Bensonvale, in Herschel.

Nana's ruminations came to an abrupt halt. The mourners were leaving, this part of the service over. She joined the line of people slowly shuffling out of the church. Outside, six double-decker buses stood waiting. Across the street from where she stood, someone beckoned to her. It was Herman. She was found!

On her way over to where he pointed, she walked past the hearse just as the chief mourners were getting into it. Her eyes shied away. She was in no hurry to see Vuyokazi's mother's eyes. The suffering she'd seen there at the wake the previous night was enough to last her a lifetime. Herman had taken her to see Mrs Rhadebe, who'd already met the other four. So, remembering the mother's agony, Nana avoided her eyes. But the glimpse of Vuyokazi's mother was enough to awaken the horror. She couldn't run away. Questions came flooding her mind, crowding out all else. How does a family deal with such grief? Her father? Was he still alive? How does something like this happen? How? Why? And the children? Her children? Were there any? Did Vuyokazi have any children? She must find out, ask. Someone was bound to know what Wayidyu-duza's situation had been . . . these days.

They had not seen each other for years. She'd married a Port Elizabeth man she met while training to be a nurse at the Livingstone Hospital. Returned to Cape Town only on short visits to her mother. She'd lost touch with all her school friends. Then, last year, Lindiwe had come to a writers' conference in P.E. She had looked her up and they had remained in touch since then. Which is how she got to know about this tragedy . . . before it made the news, that is. Got to know about it in good enough time to come to the funeral.

The shrill, insistent ringing of the phone had pulled her from deepest sleep. Eyes closed, she had reached for it, to strangle it or strangle the person on the other side. Probably some imbecile calling about a lift to the hospital. Can't complain too loudly about that, I suppose, Nana told herself. As my dear husband daily reminds me: 'they wouldn't ask if they didn't know they'd get it.'

'Hello?' She made sure to put a question mark to her voice.

'Hello? Hello, is that you, Nana?'

'Yes?'

She couldn't place the voice. But the 'Nana' meant this was someone who knew her from way back. People in P.E. called her Mrs Mdakana or, simply, MaMdakana.

The caller identified herself and they exchanged greetings.

'Ntombi!'[2] Lindiwe said. 'A terrible thing has happened here.'

'Oh!'

'D'you remember Wayidyuduza? We were at scho . . .'

'Of course, I remember her.' Fearing the worst, she rushed on, 'Don't tell me she's dead.'

Vuyokazi was one of the people she and Lindiwe had talked about. Someone she'd told herself she'd look up next time she was in Cape Town. She couldn't be dead. Too young. Her age. People her age were not dying . . . not yet. Why, even her mother was still alive.

'If it were only that,' Lindiwe said with a sigh, 'it wouldn't be so bad.'

Nana's mind whirled. What could be worse than death? Than dying? But the other's voice interrupted those thoughts.

'You'll probably hear about it in the news. Bound to. But I thought I'd let you know . . . since she and . . . since we were . . . d'you remember, how we all belonged to . . .' her voice broke.

'To the Significant Six?' Nana finished the sentence for her and then asked: 'But Lindi, what's happened to her?' She was thinking: Can't be anything political. Thank God, those hideous days are gone. No more pass arrests. No arrest on suspicion one is a terrorist. In fact, most 'terrorists' are

[2] Little girl.

119

now in government. No being fried alive on suspicion of being an informer. So, what was it? What awful thing had happened?

The next moment, she gasped, 'Oh, no! Dear God, no!' The phone receiver dropped from her hand. Her hand gone dead, ice cold, at the horror of what her ears had heard. Numb. All of her numb. A block of ice.

The clatter woke her husband, lying next to her. Seeing the phone on the floor Sandile grabbed it and hollered into the receiver, 'Hello? Hello?'

Nana didn't hear the rest of the exchange. She had sunk on to the floor. Eyes big as plates, she stared. Not a sound out of her.

And those eyes, those eyes, dry as an ancient desert grave.

◆

The hearse led the way. The buses followed close behind. A long line of cars brought up the rear. The ride with the group helped Nana a little; broke through the curtain of grief, disbelief, bewilderment.

'Barbaric!' Sidney hurled into the deafening silence in the car, opening a heated discussion.

'This is the act of cowards,' Herman hissed. 'Stupid cowards.'

'Ignorant, not stupid,' Sipho said, and added that the killers were also scared; had acted from a position of fear and ignorance.

'They were both!' hissed Lindiwe. 'Ignorant, stupid and cowardly.' All grammar forgotten, voice raised, she went on, 'Degrading her neighbourhood! Degrading her neighbourhood, indeed! What do they think they have achieved by killing her? Improved the neighbourhood? Is that it?' she sneered. 'What kind of a neighbourhood is it . . . where a woman is killed, butchered . . . by a rabid mob . . . for no other sin except telling the truth?'

'But what has happened to us? Where has our humaneness fled?' asked Sipho.

'*Ubuntu*?[3] Ha'h,' Lindiwe huffed, 'don't you see how often it is on our lips these days? Let me tell you this. Once people bandy something about all the time, it most probably has disappeared . . . or, is disappearing. It is the anxiety, the fear around its disappearance that makes them call on it, talk about it, brandish it about. There is no need to announce the obvious.'

At the cemetery, the service was short, most of it having been conducted at the church. The grave was sanctified. A prayer. The coffin lowered. As the mourners filed past the open grave, Nana saw a few faces that looked as though they might belong to people she used to know . . . had known. Of course, she could not be sure.

How strange, she thought, in his closing statement, Father Mngomeni referred to the same concept that had provoked an argument among them on the way to the cemetery: *ubuntu*.

'Like faith,' his voice firm, strong, caring, the Reverend Father had said, '*ubuntu* is not something we profess by words.' He paused, let his eyes gaze over the silent, grieving multitude.

Then he continued, 'Just as it is the actions of the individual that let us know that she or he is a person of faith,' another brief pause followed, 'so, also, is it the actions that show us when we encounter people who have *ubuntu*.'

Groans and the furious clucking of tongues punctuated the priest's words.

[3] A Zulu word; difficult to define in abstract terms, but generally meaning a social philosophy incorporating the values of personhood, humaneness, morality, honesty and concern for the social good.

121

'I do not want to judge. Nor do I want to condemn. But, let me leave you with these few words ... this thought.' His hands, palms facing, fingers pointing upward in a gesture of one in prayer, he said, 'The deed that has brought us to this place ... made us gather here ... this day ... is the deed of people singularly bereft of *ubuntu*.' Now and then as he spoke, the prayerful hands jabbed at the air for emphasis. 'The weak and vulnerable among us are not for us to harass, hound, and hunt. They are not supposed to be prey.'

A thin, despairing wail cut him short, momentarily. It had risen, as far as Nana could tell, from somewhere near the head of the grave. She guessed that was Vuyokazi's mother. Had to be. In the car she'd learnt that both her parents were still alive. Also, there was a husband and three children. Two boys and a little girl, eight years old. The boys were both in their teens. A group of women went to the aid of the keening woman and, supporting her on both sides, led her away.

With calm once more restored, the priest continued, his voice raised, the words coming faster and faster, tumbling off his lips, chasing each other: 'But, I put it to you,' he shouted, 'who is the mob who killed this young woman? Strangers? People none of us know? Aliens from outer space?

'This, my friends in Christ, is the frightening aspect of this sad case. Our sister, here, was killed by somebody's child. Somebody's friend. Somebody's brother or sister. Somebody's husband or wife. Somebody's neighbour. In short, by people we know. People we love. People who are us.'

A longish pause followed during which the priest closed his eyes. When he opened them; lightning darted from those eyes shelved under thick black brows. His voice, when he again spoke, was a loud whisper. Harsh. Fierce.

'And why did they kill her?' he asked. 'Why?' Now he looked all around him, bore into the eyes of each person present. Then, pulling the fiery eyes back to the mound of still-wet sand below which, down, deep down under it all, in the hole around which people had just filed, into which they had just thrown handfuls of sand, he answered his own question: 'They killed her only because she had the *courage* to speak the truth. She died for speaking the truth. They killed her saying she brought shame upon them. But I tell you,' he shouted, 'Vuyokazi died without shame!' Then, vigorous nodding punctuating the words, he went on, voice steadily rising all the time, 'She died free! Because she died in truth. For truth. She is free. We are the condemned. She died without shame. The shame is ours.' For a long moment, thereafter, he was silent.

'Where is our outrage?' Father Mngomeni now roared. 'Where is our outrage?' He scowled, then again was silent. Right arm raised high, he was silent. Slowly, taking his time, from one side of that large gathering his eyes travelled over the hundreds of heads. Slowly, from left to right and then back again. And then right up to the other side. Finally, he raised his arm even higher. Then, looking high above the forest of upturned heads before him, he made the sign of the cross.

◆

'Quite an inspired sermon, that minister gave,' Sipho said, heaving himself on to Lindiwe's sofa. The group had adjourned after the washing of hands and the drinking of black tea at Vuyokazi's home, following the burial service. Nana was staying with Lindiwe till her return to Port Elizabeth, on the first flight out, Monday morning.

'Eloquence is the one thing we cannot be accused of lacking, as a people,' Lindiwe shouted through the open door of her bedroom. 'The question is: what's to be done? There's been enough talk,' she said, emerging in stockings, having kicked off her shoes. 'Far too much, in fact ... Can I offer anyone anything?' she asked, going towards the kitchen, where she was joined by Nana, who had also changed into more comfortable, informal gear.

When the two women returned, each carrying a heavily-laden tray, Violet, Sidney's wife, was saying, '... that is mistake number one.'

'What did we miss?' Nana jumped in.

'I was just saying we need to be more involved in our response. Take personal responsibility and not leave things to others.'

'But my question is,' Lindiwe said, 'what to do?'

'There you go,' Violet responded. 'It's not what to do but what can I do? We must, each one of us, make the decision, the commitment, to stand up and be counted.'

'What can one person do in the face of such pervasive violence?' asked Herman.

By now, they were all seated around the spacious room, occasionally filling their plates or glasses from the platters and bottles on the table.

'I don't think that's what Violet is saying,' said Sidney.

'No, it's not!' Violet, in her own defence, added hotly. 'I am talking about individual commitment that is rooted in our allowing ourselves to be agents of change. Each person taking upon herself or himself the responsibility of visibly demonstrating, through action, the beliefs and ideals that are called for by our present situation. Nothing is going to change without the intervention, aggressive intervention at that, of more and more people. Instead of being bystanders and sympathizers, let us become active workers for change ... Because change is not going to happen of its own sweet accord.'

'I keep hearing the priest asking, "Where is your outrage?"'

124

Herman said, shaking his head, his voice barely above a whisper.

This being a Saturday afternoon, the group debated the issue well into the night. None of them were going to work the next day.

'While, like ostriches, we bury our heads in the sand,' Nana said, responding to someone's remark, 'by the year 2000,' she continued, 'not a family in South Africa will be without one member who is either HIV-positive or suffering from AIDS. Not one, according to most medical forecasts.'

Although all those present were terribly upset at what had happened to Vuyokazi, without exception, this statement from Nana, a health worker, visibly jarred them.

'You're joking?' blurted Sipho, who had so far not added much to the discussions.

Eyes solemn, Nana looked at him and said, 'Is this the face of someone in jest?'

Getting no reply, she added, 'When you play with your little daughter or son, your niece or nephew, or your grandchild, take a long look at that face and ask yourself if this is the one marked for this terrible disease? Or, is it the other? That one, perhaps? Look at the young people you love, and think about it, because one of them . . . in every family, one person . . . ONE AT LEAST, there may be more in some families . . . will die of AIDS.'

'Good God!' exclaimed Sidney, getting up and going to look out of the open window.

The gloomy prognosis had been brought home, as perhaps nothing else had that had been said earlier that day: the reality of AIDS being an epidemic, a plague, an illness that had implications not just for an anonymous face – the sad, distant someone, unknown and unknowable – but for each and everyone in the country. Without exception. Implications for each one of them in that very room. If not themselves, then someone they knew, someone they loved, would be stricken by it. It was not a question of if, maybe, or perhaps, but when? And who?

'Unless we act,' said Violet, her gaze on her husband's hunched shoulders. 'Unless we act and act aggressively. NOW!'

'We have already lost a friend to AIDS and ignorance about AIDS,' Sipho said, looking morose. 'What more incentive do we need?'

The next couple of hours were spent in planning, scheming, weighing this and that option, identifying groups to target or enlist (including departments of government). Lists were made, songs written, colours chosen, slogans minted.

It was determined that each person present, according to what talents they possessed, commit themselves to joining the fight against AIDS. What is more, they were to keep in touch, share news of progress, share strategies, successes and handicaps encountered. But work they must.

They parted late that night and met again, for a few hours, the next day. More work. More plans. They also spent some time catching up on each other's lives, marvelling at what they had become, how the prophecy of the Significant Six had been realized. They mourned their recent loss, bid good-bye to Nana, and promised to keep in touch, now that fate had once more brought them together.

Sandile was waiting for her at the airport, early that Monday morning. He gave her a warm embrace and, arm in arm, they walked to the car. He opened the door for her, went round to the driver's side and got in. He inserted the key and then, brows pleated, turned to her and asked, 'What's with the red ribbon?'

Fingering the ribbon on her left shoulder, Nana smiled. 'This shows that I'm a member of AIDS-SA.' She did not elaborate.

126

'I'm sure you'll tell me all about it, before we get home?' he teased.

'Here's your ribbon,' and, with that, she fished the red satin bow from her pocket and pinned it on his chest. 'This is how we've decided to honour Vuyokazi's memory. By identifying ourselves publicly with the struggle against AIDS. We're to start a branch here in P.E.'

'We are?' But his chuckle belied the question.

As the car pulled out of the parking lot, Nana reached to the back seat, yanked her bag over, opened it and took out a notebook. 'Let me read this out to you. See how it sounds,' and amidst Sandile's occasional grunts of approval, she proceeded to read from the notes she had made on the plane.

'Well thought out, I must say,' he said when the reading stopped. 'But, will it work?' And before she'd said a word in response, he added, 'Sounds ambitious.'

'My darling,' Nana replied, head nodding her determination, 'like laughter, enthusiasm can be infectious. We must infect the whole country with this idea that AIDS is not next door. It is right on our threshold, on our doorstep, peeping through our windows, lifting the blankets off our beds, and revealing our nakedness. Concerted and aggressive action is called for. We need the will to survive, the will to do what we must do to stay alive.'

'Count me in!'

'Why d'you think I pinned that ribbon on your chest?' she replied. 'There's only one way to beat this devil. Action! That is how.'

127

CHIEDZA MUSENGEZI

Crocodile Tails

Secondary schools swelled with pupils: young mothers who had prematurely terminated their studies, those who had fought in the War of Liberation, and truants who had been expelled, were all given a second chance. These grown people sat with their backs bent double over small desks built for twelve-year-olds. They all believed education meant a better life. The rectangular metal sheet, erected at the main entrance, bore the school motto: 'He who rejects education rejects good living.' It was quite clear who was going to benefit in the newly independent Zimbabwe. Newspapers, radios, and parents echoed the same message. Teachers pocketed monthly wages – decent and liveable ones – that equalled those of our local white counterparts. It had never happened before.

We used the word 'expat' to describe the foreign, expatriate teachers. 'Expat teachers, *amaexpats*.' Expatriate teachers.

There was an unwritten rule at Nkulumane that in the staff room one should always sit in the same chair. The longer your stay in the school, the more your chair would be left alone. Your space was well defined. The new teachers did not appear anchored, they floated from one chair to the next before they eventually established their sitting places. Thereafter, every day, I found myself sitting next to one of the British teachers, Gill.

Gill, therefore, was my first close contact with the West. Even though she was British, she was warm, humble and had soft eyes which said she was eager to mix. First, we exchanged the morning greetings. Soon, we progressed to more friendly gestures; offering to pour each other a cup of tea, extending a hand with a piece of bread or a newspaper.

It was Gill's absence from school for three successive days that drew me closer to her. Nobody knew what the matter was. Some of the expats claimed the food they ate in the cafés upset their digestive system. Some reacted badly to mosquito bites, and an afternoon in the sun left others with faces red and tender like over-ripe tomatoes. Their bodies needed to go back home but they spoke of how marvellously they were coping. In spirit they were at home, and their physical discomfort seemed an inconvenience but not a problem. I thought Gill was ill, so on my way home, I stopped by her apartment in town.

Gill was sitting on her bed. A thick novel, *The Thorn Birds*, lay face down. She looked surprised but pleased to see me. Her face lit up.

'*Sakubona*.'[1]

She had made an effort to learn the local language and I had tried to help her. But we had soon given up. We were both impatient. Meaningful conversation is what we wanted. Our Ndebele conversation hardly rose above baby talk. Gill mastered single isolated words that could not make a sentence. *Bhala* – write, *hlala* – sit, and so on and so forth.

'What's wrong? Why are you not reporting for work?' I asked.

'Nothing really, I'll be back tomorrow.' She sounded grave.

I did not press her for details. I was not sure if we were close enough to talk about our personal lives. Gill made some tea, and showed me some photographs which she must have been looking at when I arrived. She picked up the album from her bed. They were photographs of her parents, cousins, aunts, and uncles. Some were of herself at college in the physics

[1] Hello.

129

laboratory, looking at objects through a magnifying lens. One was of a hi-fi system she said she had assembled with her own hands.

'This is my father,' she said, pointing at a balding man with a smile.

He was an industrialist, the manager of an electronics company. She showed me more but my eyes lingered on the photograph of a small girl standing between a man and a woman. Gill at five years. Her little face shone with cleanliness, her skirt, heavily gathered at the waist and trimmed with lace, stood out like an umbrella. Everything about her revealed that she was a protected and treasured child. But now she looked sad.

A young white woman from a rich family, with a sound education; what was her problem?

'Why are you here if you're so unhappy?'

'To teach physics, but . . . also to achieve something personal. I want to experience hardship.'

Her reply silenced me.

'My life has been too easy,' she said. 'A steadily flowing stream – no ripples. I want greater problems. Challenges. I want to be hardened by pain and experience, like you.'

Confusion spread over my face, a twitch on my lips soon spread into a giggle. Rejecting comfort? Here I was, struggling to provide my children with all that I had longed to have in my childhood: a bed, a pair of shoes, tea, bread.

'Well, the pain and experience won't be fun,' I pointed out.

Gill objected. She desired to be like me. She wanted to struggle to improve herself; she wanted to do so alone without the assistance of her parents. She was disappointed that she had found no hardships in Zimbabwe. She had expected to be posted to a rural school where she would have had to carry a bucket of water from a borehole, cook over a smoky fire and wait for hours for a bus to town.

She was living in the city, Bulawayo, because most schools that offered A-level physics were in the cities.

'What is the point in leaving home to come to Africa and living as if I were in England? Well, almost,' she corrected herself. She was planning to return at the end of the year to further her studies at Oxford University.

Although Gill was not enjoying herself, the rest of the foreign teachers were having the time of their lives. They were different from the white people we had always known. They rented houses in the African townships of Mzilikazi, Luveve and Nkulumane in Bulawayo. They walked the township streets without fear, leaving behind them a trail of startled but delighted children screaming, '*Amakiwa! Amakiwa!*'[2] They did not drive themselves to work. We met up at the bus station. In the queue we both patiently waited in all types of weather – the October heat and January rain. At school, the pupils loved them. They were not severe disciplinarians. They were very knowledgeable in their subject areas, particularly English literature and the sciences. While most of us – the local teachers – harassed and bullied the pupils with insults and ridicule, the expat teachers praised the pupils' humble efforts.

'You are struggling against great odds,' they told them. 'With a single textbook between ten of you, and studying all your subjects in English . . . You are doing fine. And did you know that the Cambridge O-level exam is meant to select the top twenty-five percent of any given population?'

For the first time in their lives the pupils learnt that three-quarters of them were meant to fail. The new teachers were surprised to experience classroom practices that had long been outlawed in their countries.

Tom Buchanan, the teacher from Australia whose classroom

---

[2] White people.

was next to Mrs Ngwenya's, listened with disapproval as she raged at her Form 3 pupils for failing their biology test.

'Looking at you, one would think you're First Grade seed. You look bright enough from the outside. But, if I were to put you in water you would all float. You are chaff! You have nothing but empty heads.'

She and the rest of us local teachers sent pupils to the headmaster for failing their tests. The headmaster would make them bend over a chair and thrash them with a bamboo rod. The expat teachers hardly ever sent the pupils who failed their tests for flogging. They refused to write notes on the chalk-board for their classes to copy into exercise books. Rote and drill were old and ineffectual teaching styles, they said. They did not believe in policing pupils, so exercise books were not marked frequently. Self-discipline – teaching the pupils responsibility – that was their way.

The headmaster looked at them with concern. A challenge or trial? Never in his life had he dreamt of having so many whites working under him. Sure, it was a sign of the new independent Zimbabwe.

The pupils took advantage. They gave excuses for missing lessons and not handing in their written work. They turned up late in the morning.

'The bus left us,' some said.

'No, the bus didn't leave you, you missed it,' the expat teachers corrected with a hint of annoyance.

The students became noisy in class. They whined about how unreasonable the local teachers were. Nearly a quarter of Gill's all-male physics class had not done a stroke of work for a whole term.

'They are grown men. Handsome, tasteful ones too,' Gill said, almost laughing. 'They ought to know what they are doing.'

Two terms into the school year, we exchanged observations about our new workmates. The expat teachers were lax, permissive even. They spared the rod and spoiled the children. These were Zimbabwean children. Where on earth were these new teachers preparing our children to live? Europe? It was not surprising when Mr Moyo brought up the matter for discussion in one of the weekly staff meetings.

The expat teachers argued against flogging. It was humiliating, they said. Beatings instilled fear. A healthy respect for authority, a situation that allowed them to voice their concerns without fear was all the pupils required. Children had rights. The new freedoms in independent Zimbabwe were for everybody, children included.

We knew about political independence. 'One man, one vote,' was a slogan we had all chanted before. 'Child rights' were new. We, the local teachers, disagreed, looked to the headmaster to have the final say. He was relieved that we trusted him to support us. For a while he had felt his firm hold over his school loosen. He was locked in a battle of his own about what to do: reprimand the new teachers and risk the pupils labelling him a racist dictator, or leave the situation as it was and risk the teachers calling him a black coward, scared of exercising authority over whites? He cleared his throat. He was firm and sharp, and seized the opportunity to exert his authority.

'The pupils have exams to sit at the end of the year. Exercise books must be marked. Pupils who do not do their work must be sent to my office.'

The matter was closed. He paused for effect before running his eyes along the front row where the expat teachers were sitting.

The meeting left an unpleasant aftertaste. However, nobody dwelt on it for long. It was frank and honest, some commented.

The new teachers censored their speech during staff meetings. Consequences of actions, inside and outside the classroom, were mulled over beforehand. They had tested the limits and they now knew how far they could go. They wrote copious notes on the board for pupils to copy into their exercise books, and turned a deaf ear to the cries of pain from the pupils who got lashed. They blamed the beatings on cultural differences.

Once, both of us – the local and expat teachers – exchanged glances as we walked past some students, who, with hands raised in the air, knelt on the tarmac for hours. The headmaster had punished them for coming late to school. The sight of them left all of us ill at ease. It was disturbing. They resembled pumpkin vines wilting in the midday sun.

Gill remained cool and silent, refusing to be drawn into the argument. It was not her place, she told me, to instruct Zimbabweans on how to behave. Besides, she was looking for greater problems to absorb her unused energies.

School holidays provided a time to travel, and she joined the group on their travels around the country. Armed with their cameras, binoculars, backpacks and hard currency, they explored the game parks throughout the country: Hwange, Gonarezhou, Matopos, Chizarira. In the hotels and night-clubs, they ordered beer and wine and tried exotic dishes like *sadza* and crocodile tail. They danced with local young men and women to the local bands: the Bhundu Boys, Munya Brown and Thomas Mapfumo. When schools opened for the next term, they brought back big envelopes, fat with photographs. They enthusiastically passed them round at tea-time in the staff room for all to see. They gasped, again, at the full-colour pictures of a leopard resting on the branch of a tree, at a herd of buffalo, and at the impalas grazing in the wild. Sometimes there were photographs of the Matopos, showing rocks and boulders piled high upon each other. I was not enthusiastic about the photos. What was there to see if they had no people in them? The beauty of the pristine wild was beyond me.

Gill left for Britain at the end of the year. We wrote to each other regularly. Two years later, I scraped together enough money as a down payment on one of the 'Fly Now, Pay Later' schemes. The announcement of my intended trip drew comments from my envious friends.

'You'll bring back nice clothes. A colour television and computer.'

'Bring back pounds and make money when you change them at the bank.'

'You'll come back looking prettier, your skin tone will be light from the cold.'

A trip to the West meant transformation for the better. Where was I going to acquire enough sterling to go shopping and bring back home enough change to take to the bank? But I did not say anything; instead, I glowed in their baseless envy.

At Heathrow Airport I collected my luggage and wheeled my trolley. I followed the arrows pointing to the customs clearance hall. Soon I was standing before a customs official; uniformed, hard-faced, clean-shaven, with closely cropped hair and a commanding voice. He let loose an avalanche of questions.

'Why are you here? Holiday or business?

'Who are you visiting?

'How long have you known each other?

'Does your friend have a job?

'What is her address?

'Do you have family? Property?'

There was no end to what he wanted to know. I must have answered the questions to his satisfaction for he banged my passport with a rubber stamp. In the arrival hall, Gill was waiting. In a crowd of white faces I could not distinguish hers. She spotted me and waved wildly.

We were walking across the tarmac of the carport when I looked up. My eyes met up with a grey sky which hung so low I could almost touch it.

MONDE SIFUNISO

Night Thoughts

As I lie here in bed, I wonder what time it is. The ward is dimly lit, and the night nurse is asleep at her table. The patient directly opposite my bed has been in a coma for a week. The other two patients on her side of the ward are quiet, at last. Earlier in the evening one had been delirious, and the other had been moaning and calling for a doctor who never came. The patient next to me is dead except for her head. She can open and close her eyes, she can move her head and even attempt to speak. But that is all she can do.

The night is silent, and tonight I feel no pain. Tonight I can cast my thoughts over the last three years that you have been away. I can see you now, your fingers pulling absently at your scanty beard, a small knowing smile on your lips, your eyes looking into distances that my naked eyes could not see. Had you told me, that last day I saw you, that I would not be seeing you for a long time, I would have stayed a little longer with you.

When you left, Sikiti was the *litunga* of Barotseland, our head of state. He was already unpopular by that time, remember? I'm sure you remember how he was pelted with rotten oranges and tomatoes when he tried to address students at Tukuluho University. He was lucky no one could afford to throw an egg at his pate.

Three months after your departure Sikiti had the decency to abdicate. There was much rejoicing everywhere. Total strangers hugged and swung each other round. We even had a fireworks display. The royal committee did not waste time.

137

Within three days that cocky son of that other unpopular *litunga*, nicknamed Mutelo, was installed in Sikiti's place. As per tradition, he was installed outside the *kuta*, in front of the palace. He took the name Liswani and became Liswani II. We were short-sighted enough to become excited and extol him. He became a giant of a man in our minds.

For a week or so there was euphoria in the capital. We did nothing but stare dreamy-eyed at him on television screens as he promised us what Sikiti had taken away from us – heaven on earth. He was so eloquent that when he told us of the succulent steaks we would be eating again we did not only see them in our minds' eyes, but we could hear them sizzling and smell them as well. Here was a *litunga* who shared our hopes for the future, who was opposed to some of the retrogressive customs of our country, and encouraged free thinking. Liswani II became the first *litunga* to talk about democracy in our monarchy. I admit, I, too, allowed myself to be carried away on a wave of optimism.

After the mandatory two weeks, King Liswani moved into the palace. He stopped on the last step and waved at us before he stepped into that stately home. He was barely inside for a minute before he shot out like a bullet to tell us that someone had carried away all but the bricks and mortar of the palace! It did not mean that, just because he wanted to work himself to the bone for his country, he did not need a chair to sit on, or a bed to sleep in. In that short moment he was in the palace he had managed to peep into the treasury, and he told us that Sikiti had left the coffers of the nation empty. Can you believe that I was ready to take up a collection for him? Maybe some people did, because the very following week some trucks trundled over from Namiba, and off-loaded the most expensive furniture that you've ever seen. In the meantime, our efficient police force has not yet found out who carted away the palace furniture.

It did not take us long to realize that, even though the 'Nalikwanda', the royal barge, now had an engine and did not need to be paddled, nothing else had changed. Liswani changed his title officially from *litunga* to king. The *ngambela* became the prime minister; the *kuta* became the cabinet, and his *indunas* became cabinet ministers! *Induna Kalonga* became minister of education, *Induna Mukwakwa* became minister of works and supply, and so on and so forth. In came Land Rovers and the latest four-wheel-drive vehicles for the new king and his ministers. Down went our living conditions. Back came the arrogance of the Sikiti era. Anyone who complained was labelled an enemy of the state and was arrested. This was new. If there is anything we have had plenty of in our country, even during Sikiti's reign, it's free speech. *Mulena ki mutangaa sicaba*, went our saying – 'the king is the servant of the nation'. Now Liswani erected a barrier between the royal family and the people. He began to abuse the *litunga*'s habit of going incognito among the people to find out what they thought about him. In the past, the information gathered in these nightly prowls helped the *litungas* shape themselves to the people's expectations. The new king who loved free thinkers arrested people who said things he considered demeaning even if they were said in drunken stupors.

When King Liswani closed the royal channel of communication, we turned to the grapevine for information. I don't know how much of what I have heard over the last three years is true and how much is fabrication. Some stories were credible; some I took with a pinch of salt; others I dismissed outright. I mean, if you're given a graphic description, not by one person but by several, of how someone close to the king himself killed a man, you will believe it. When you're told that a prominent person's wife is threatening to leave him because a poltergeist is creating havoc in their lofty abode, you're not sure whether to believe it or laugh in the face of the narrator; only there was always more than one informant. But when people swear to you that in the palace there is a room holding some of our dead *litungas* in zombie state, and that the same room boasts a photograph that bleeds, then you know imaginations are running wild.

Then came the most incredible of all the rumours. Liswani II was going mad, losing his mind. Why? He was haunted by a living man, his predecessor, Sikiti. It was said that one night, King Liswani retired to bed at the normal time. He didn't know what woke him up, but when he opened his eyes he saw Sikiti sitting in a chair by his bed. He reacted in an infantile way. He pulled his bedclothes over his head and screamed. The queen's bedroom is separated from the king's by a door. Soon after his coronation the king had locked that door, and he had kept it locked because his national responsibilities took precedence over his conjugal ones. So, on this night, by the time the queen had scrambled out of bed and gone round to the door that opened into the passageway – the door the king was not in the habit of locking – the bodyguards were already there opening wardrobes and looking under the bed. The king was sitting quaking on the bed. She sat next to him and quietly asked what was going on.

'Sikiti,' her husband pushed the name through clenched teeth.

'Here?' she asked incredulously. No one answered her. Everyone knew that Sikiti had left for South Africa the previous day.

The king was now at a loss as to what to do. He reasoned that, if his bedroom door had been locked that night, his bodyguards would not have managed to come to his rescue. Yet it was because the door had not been locked that Sikiti had managed to slip into his room. In the end, he decided to lock that door as well, turning his bedroom into a cocoon where only one special cleaner was allowed.

During Sikiti's reign our relations with Zambia had soured. Liswani was determined to restore the good neighbourliness that had existed between the two countries.

One night, Liswani flew back from a peace-making trip to Zambia, exhausted. He dismissed all questions and promised that he'd call a press conference the following day. What we heard afterwards was that he went to his private study first and had some discussions with his press secretary. After his press secretary had left, he sat down to read a book, and fell asleep in his chair. When he woke up, Sikiti was sitting in a chair opposite him, holding the book the king had been reading.

It is now treasonable to mention what happened next, but since you won't repeat this, I'll tell you. The king soiled his pants and passed out. The theory then was that the stench activated the alarm system. When the king was located he was found neatly laid out on the floor, his hands crossed on his chest like yesterday's corpse. That was when the psychiatrist was brought in and, later, a priest to exorcize whoever had possessed our *litunga*. It could not be Sikiti. He had left Barotseland for Botswana two days before the king claimed he had seen him in his study.

You know that in spite of all the fun we make of our *litungas* we are basically a very loyal people. When we realized that the king was genuinely ill, we rallied behind him. We started searching for something good in him. It was difficult, but our hearts warmed to him when we saw his eyes crinkle childishly in laughter again. We were happy as the carefree gait he had lost returned to his step.

Our king enjoyed adulation for four months. Then disaster struck again. One afternoon, King Liswani went into the palace library and found Sikiti setting up a chess board on the coffee table. He ran out of there, lashing out at anyone who tried to stop him. He was halfway to the gate before a daring guard tripped him. He refused to be led back into the palace. The king and the queen were moved to one of the smaller houses behind the palace, the houses that were once used by the *litungas'* junior wives (when it was mandatory for a *litunga* to have five wives). However, the king continued to conduct his business from the main house. This time Sikiti had been seen leaving the house of the minister of home affairs, just after the king had run helter-skelter from the palace. When questioned, the minister vehemently denied that ex-king Sikiti had visited him.

One October morning, the *litunga* called his cabinet to a meeting. While they were having tea at ten o'clock, he excused himself and left the room. An hour later, he had not returned. His private secretary was sent to find out whether the meeting was over. He came back to report that he had not found him. After establishing that the king had not driven out, the ministers quietly searched the palace. Two hours later it was clear that the king was neither in the palace nor in the other houses within the palace walls. A search of the spacious grounds yielded nothing.

At the palace gate the names of all the people who had driven out between ten and eleven o'clock were taken. They were located and summoned to the palace. They all denied driving out with the king hidden in their cars. Now that the five men and one woman knew about the disappearance of the king they had to be kept at the palace. Two of the men had no phones in their homes, so someone had to go to their homes to reassure their families that they were safe and sound. One of the men's wives panicked. She told the editor of *Koranta*, a notorious tabloid, that her husband had been arrested. When the story was shouted from the front page of the paper the following day, the wives of several ministers (who had also had to spend the night at the palace) started a frantic search for their husbands. The result was that, by lunch time, everyone knew that the king had disappeared.

Now came reports of sightings! The king was seen in Senanga. The police there organized themselves and searched . . . Sesheke, Kalabo, Lukulu . . . nothing. On the third day the minister of home affairs was having lunch with three members of the royal committee.

'If the king has not returned by tomorrow your committee will have to meet and decide what to do,' the minister said.

'We could say he abdicated because of the problems he has been having,' said one of the members of the royal commitee.

'This is a good example of divine intervention. Spirited away in a UFO,' another member said.

'Don't fire the people's imaginations with stories of UFOs. They'll report seeing him jumping over the moon,' a third member said.

'The moon is one place he should avoid if he is sensible. It's no place for lunatics,' the minister said amid laughter from the other three.

'It's interesting to know what people think of you,' the unmistakable voice of the king said as he walked into the room wearing the same clothes he had been wearing at their last meeting.

The minister of home affairs and his guests scrambled to their feet and attempted to show how happy they were to see him. He glanced sideways at them and curled his upper lip as though he were looking at fleas on a mongrel's back. He picked up a cellphone that was on the sideboard and walked out of the room. They heard him speak on the phone but they could

143

not catch what he was saying. They sat there, not even looking at each other, unsure what they should do.

When they heard a car turn into the minister's gate, they all sighed. They needed a distraction. When the car stopped, they expected the king to rush in and hide. When that didn't happen, the minister got up to find out who had come. He was in time to see the king get into a palace car and drive off without a backward glance. He had no choice but to call his guests and follow Liswani to the palace. However, the king had left instructions not to allow them, or any members of his cabinet, in. They were turned away right at the gate. For the next five days, word that the palace was a hive of activity reached every ear.

'Liswani is up to no good,' the minister of home affairs said to himself. He dared not voice these sentiments to anyone. People could not trust even their spouses now that Liswani paid so handsomely for information on what people said about him.

Six days after his reappearance, Liswani called a press conference. All his ministers were to be present. Members of the diplomatic corps were expected to attend. For the first time, members of the extended royal family were also invited. And, for the first time also, no rumours preceded the press conference. We were all mystified. Don't ask me how I found myself at the palace that day, but there I was, along with the very best, the curious and the concerned!

King Liswani came out wearing his royal regalia. He looked proud and dignified. I saw in him a touch of that great ancestor of his, King Lewanika. He sat on his throne, on the podium, and became his petty self again.

'Here I am, ladies and gentlemen, to the chagrin of my detractors. Today I'm going to expose my enemies, and the enemies of our country, because anyone who wishes me ill, wishes the country ill.' He gave a mirthless laugh.

While he was giving this introductory talk a giant screen was being set up. In the middle of a sentence a wall appeared on the screen. As though we were watching a modern-day Alice in Wonderland, we saw a woman reporter touch the wall. As she turned round to beckon to people who were still out of the picture, a chink appeared in the wall. Four other reporters walked up to the first reporter while the king himself took up the rear. In single file, they walked to the aperture and passed through the wall. They had walked into the palace's private garden. We were shown a small gate that opened out to the road behind, but it was covered by beautiful climbers that concealed it completely. The group then walked towards the palace and stood by a manhole. They removed the manhole cover and all six of them descended into . . . well . . . the sewer. However, the next shot showed steps that went down to a huge pipe where all of them could stand upright. They walked through this pipe and climbed through another manhole, into the garden of the minister of home affairs.

'You will recall that Sikiti's son used to live in that house, and had to be forcibly removed after my installation. Now we know why. Many of you, including the people I picked up from the ashes to run the affairs of the nation with me, went around shouting that Liswani was mad, Liswani was mad.'

There was silence. Even the court jesters were quiet.

'You were all on Sikiti's side, and you were ready to testify that each time I claimed to have seen him, he was out of the country. As you can see, he simply went underground. The question that each intelligent person should ask is, why was it necessary for Sikiti to have a secret passage to his son's house?

'Countrymen, this passage was not built by Sikiti and his son alone. There are men, and women, who knew about the passage, who laboured to build it, but even when my sanity was being questioned, no one came forward to tell me that

145

there was a possibility that Sikiti could get into the palace without being seen.

'Sikiti is out of the country now, tipped off by someone to run away. He will return, and he will have a lot of questions to answer when he does. His son is under arrest, and he is already helping the police in their investigations. I now wish to publicly commend the Mutai Group of Companies which worked night and day over the last week to seal that passage.'

Where was Liswani when Sikiti was *litunga*? Of course there was no official announcement, but we knew about the making of the underground passage, didn't we? I even recall how you and I discussed Lewanika's escape in 1884, when there was a rebellion against him: how Lewanika's enemies, having been assured that Lewanika was in bed, stormed the palace. There was evidence that Lewanika had slept in his bed, but he was not in the bedroom nor anywhere else in the palace. Mataa and his fellow turncoats could not understand how Lewanika had escaped because they had sealed every exit. Lewanika safely reached Angola.

Well, Liswani has sealed Sikiti's method of ensuring that a *litunga* could escape if the people rose against him, though it was not a very intelligent plan to run to his son's house in an uprising. King Liswani said nothing about those three days. Did Sikiti hold Liswani prisoner? Was Sikiti truly out of the country? For now, the king turned his wrath on his *indunas*, rather, his ministers.

'I have decided to get a new team to work with me, people who have consistently shown faith in me.'

Oh, my! Now he truly showed how mad he was. He appointed new ministers and a new prime minister. One by one he castigated the outgoing cabinet. What were they but a bunch of ungrateful spongers? I was afraid to stand up and leave, and that was really when my headaches started, or that was when I became aware of them. I kept mentioning this incident to each doctor I saw, and each said that I shouldn't take national issues so personally. I was stressing myself needlessly.

If things were bad before, now they became unbearable. The group of inexperienced louts around Liswani were interested in enriching themselves more than the previous lot. Prices of everything shot up. Few people could afford even one decent meal a day. Many of us lost our jobs as the job market shrank. The situation became desperate. How could anyone tell me not to worry? I don't want to dwell on this. My head has started throbbing.

Perhaps it really was because of these problems that my headaches became so acute that my sight became affected, and I often screamed with pain, like a child. Finally I was referred to Lewanika Hospital. By sheer coincidence there was a visiting neurosurgeon. He took a look at me and immediately said that I should be admitted. He told the doctors he was with, in my hearing, that he suspected I had a brain tumour. A few tests confirmed this. The tumour was malignant and it was in an advanced stage. I didn't have long to live, I was told.

The prognosis cheered me. The tumour is the only thing I possess, the only thing I can call my own. The suffering I see around me gnaws at my heart. The pain I feel as hunger slices my entrails far exceeds the pain I should be feeling as the tumour ravages my brain. I'm losing my sight, and I sometimes hear myself screaming. My voice is disembodied. Maybe I only whimper weakly. I can no longer tell.

You've not communicated with me in the last three years. Now that I'll be with you soon, please assure me that there is no pain, no hunger after death, and that we'll be laughing together again, even as we leap about trying to find a cooler place between the licking tongues of the fires of hell. It will be heaven compared to what Barotseland has become.

GUGU NDLOVU

The Barrel of a Pen

The hotel was a pre-war building. I don't remember what it was called. It stood at the corner of two wide streets across from the Bulawayo train station, the only rail connection between Lusaka and Harare. You could hear the train's whistle slice the afternoon silence. As we approached, a sun-wilted woman sat on a newspaper selling her wares – biscuits, sweets, cigarettes and matches – from a chipped enamel basin. Two of her barefoot children played a game of train with cardboard boxes in an alley, while her third child, snotty-nosed and just crawling, tasted a cabbage leaf she had found at my feet. I stepped over her into the chilling shadow of the hotel.

Hesitating, I tapped a diseased silver bell covered with rust spots on the desk. The 'ting' disturbed some flies that buzzed hungrily around a greasy brown paper lying near it. On the wall behind the desk, a calendar with a picture of Miss July, a blonde in a polka-dot thong bikini, hung crookedly. Next to Miss July a large industrial nail held up the corner of tattered velvet curtain, which half-heartedly concealed an entrance that I assumed led back to an office.

A middle-aged Indian man whose skin emanated a sickly yellow hue emerged from behind the velvet. Deep pockmarks from old acne scars puckered the skin in his cheeks. His beady eyes made me feel naked as they sought the curve of my bosom. I shivered in disgust as an image of his hard yellow curry cock behind the counter came to mind.

'We need a room for an hour,' I said, sounding a bit too angry as I tried to conceal my embarrassment. I was pretty sure the people seeing the three of us enter the hotel must have thought we were prostitutes, known to frequent the establishment.

Rachel and Ntando wandered into the hotel lounge.

I secured the key.

Township music blended with the sound of drunken voices, loud obnoxious laughter and cigarette smoke. The lounge, as it was called, seemed more like a bar, a place where prostitutes began the process of entertaining customers while enticing others.

'Dabt bwill bwe fifteen dolur,' Rajah said. I read his name off the breast pocket of his sweat-stained uniform. I withdrew a tattered twenty-dollar bill out of my purse. Refusing to make eye-contact, I held out the bill for him and carefully examined a hangnail on my thumb. His yellow bloodshot eyes sought my face and chest as he snatched the twenty.

In exchange for the money he placed a key in my hand with a small piece of cardboard tied to it. 33 was scrawled on it in black felt-tip pen. As he did this, he purposefully brushed his sweaty hand against mine. His other hand remained behind the counter. I imagined he was fondling himself, as there was the consistent sound of jingling keys.

Suddenly grabbing my hand, he looked at me directly and said, 'Yew ur berri beawtiful, I'd love tew see yew in a chower nayked maybe . . .' Before he could finish a shrill woman's voice angrily exploded from behind the curtain in an indecipherable dialect. Red-faced and puffy, he yelled back in the same language and disappeared behind the curtain telling the woman he was sick and tired of her cooking.

Seeing this as my chance to escape, I forgot my change and quickly turned towards the lounge. I found Rachel and Ntando smoking nervously at the bar and drinking Cokes. A third Coke sat untouched beside an empty chair.

'I didn't know what you wanted so I ordered you a Coke,' Rachel said without looking up from the bar top.

I knew she was scared as shit, but if I didn't know her as well as I did, I would never have been able to tell. In all the fourteen years that I'd known her, I'd never seen her cry. Even when her little brother had been killed by a 'hit-and-run' two years ago, she had never shed a tear.

We had only met Ntando a few days ago. We had found her through Tanya, a high-school friend from a few years back. Although she was our junior she had hung out with us. I didn't like Ntando. She had a nervousness about her that was hard to trust. But in our situation we didn't have much choice. We had no money, and we were desperate. I believe Tanya must have been one of Ntando's best customers; she had used her at least five times in the past three years.

'Drink lots of fluids,' Ntando said to Rachel. Rachel glanced at Ntando and took a long puff of her cigarette.

We drank in silence. The Coke tasted like syrupy water. Rachel lit up another cigarette with the butt of the first. She tapped her fingers on the table.

'A shot of brandy to calm your nerves,' I suggested.

We ordered two brandies from the bartender, a young guy about our age with unkempt hair and a bad set of cross-eyes.

'Ten dollars,' he said, facing Rachel, although he was really looking at me.

'The last time I drank brandy must have been at Sean's party,' Rachel said, as she handed the bartender a ten-dollar bill.

'Don't you remember we finished that bottle at the pool last weekend?' I said, trying to sound sympathetic. It had occurred to me that her fear might have given her a temporary memory lapse.

'That wasn't brandy,' Rachel said as she gulped down her

drink. 'This here is brandy, that stuff you got last week tasted like your gogo's piss,' she added, as she slammed the empty glass to the counter and looked at me with a smirk.

I guess she hadn't forgotten. I was notorious for buying cheap liquor, and often paid the consequences with terrible hangovers and relentless taunting from party mates.

'Agh, Rachel man, leave my granny alone, how would you know what her piss tastes like anyway?' I replied with mock annoyance. Perhaps I was worrying about her too much.

'Eh, Squinty, get me two beers,' a scrawny-looking prostitute yelled, waving a crisp one-hundred-dollar bill over Ntando's head. She sat in the lap of a fat man and casually ashed his cigarette for him on to the floor.

'What kind?' the bartender asked, facing the prostitute but looking at the top of Rachel's hair.

'Castle,' she replied. She was wearing a tight skimpy minidress, enhancing the small curve of her tiny breasts and the angular shape of her bony buttocks.

Someone pushed me from behind and the brandy went up my nose. My eyes watered and I was blinded with my own tears. Behind me I could hear two men arguing in Ndebele mixed with English.

'I'll kill you!' the fat man's voice bellowed directly behind me. My heart skipped a beat, and I looked up at Squinty who had a curious grin on his face. His face was turned towards the scene. His eyes contained the excitement of the drama that was occurring but seemed transfixed on my forehead.

I turned to Rachel and Ntando. 'Let's go,' I said, looking at my watch. 'We have forty-five minutes.'

As we approached the exit, there was the sound of smashing glass as the fat man fell backwards through a low lounge table. The buttons on his shirt had come undone and his large fleshy stomach lay exposed. His flesh rippled in waves as his body settled from the fall. Then the crowd seemed to swallow him.

Rachel and Ntando followed me down the dark, narrow hallway that led to the room. We walked in silence. The chaos of the bar became faint and muffled, and the sound of Ntando's plastic shopping bag dominated the air as it rustled amid our footsteps.

Room thirty-three was situated at the end of the long corridor. It wasn't as unpleasant as I had imagined. It had a small single bed with clean sheets on it. In the corner there was a sink, and clean towels hung on the rack next to it. The window looked out into the alley where the children had been playing trains. But it was empty now. I closed the curtain.

Ntando removed the barrel of an Eversharp ball-point pen and a large bag of pink cotton balls from her bag and placed them on the bed. Her whole demeanour changed. The nervous energy left her and she became commanding and authoritative. It was a relief.

Later I understood her nervousness. It wasn't about doing the job, as I had thought, but about getting caught. She had worked as a nurse's aide in the hospital and had watched the procedure performed hundreds of times – there was no doubt that she knew what she was doing.

'Take off your panties,' she said.

Rachel removed them and flung them next to her purse. Next she unpinned the folded cloth that was tightly bound around her waist. A few weeks earlier I had noticed the slight bulge in her waistline and suggested she bind it, since she had no intention of having the baby.

Spreading one of the towels over the bedspread, she indicated to Rachel to hoist up her skirt and lie on the towel. I felt quite queasy as I went to lock the door. I placed the only chair in the room in front of it and sat down.

THE BARREL OF A PEN

From where I sat I could see the back of Rachel's head and her bare thighs. Ntando seemed to emerge from between Rachel's legs.

As I pondered over whether or not I could stay in the room there was the sound of keys in our door. We all looked at each other and froze. If it were the police we would all go to jail for at least ten years. Surely the police wouldn't open the door; they would bang on it and demand us to open it. Maybe it was the receptionist. I cracked open the now unlocked door to the startled faces of a man and a woman.

'What are you doing?' I asked angrily, as I stepped out into the hallway.

'This is our room,' the man said calmly in an American accent.

'There must have been a mix-up,' I said, showing them our key.

'Why does this always happen to us?' the woman sighed, dropping her backpack to the floor in annoyance. I noticed her red sunburnt shoulders. She wore a white undervest without a bra. Hippies, I thought to myself.

'Well, we'll be checking out within the next hour or so. I suggest you go down and talk to the receptionist about the matter,' I said as politely as I could. 'You know how these cheap hotels operate,' I added, trying to sound as friendly as possible.

'Yeah,' the guy responded, as he pushed a loose strand of hair back behind his ear. 'I guess you get what you pay for.'

I listened to the flopping of their Birkenstocks on the stairs before re-entering the room.

Feeling less queasy, I settled back into the chair and thought of Rachel's baby inside her. Oblivious to what was about to happen. It was almost four months. The doctor had said it was a girl and quite active. He was a foreign doctor – German, I think. He said he would do it, then refused but kept the 2000 dollars we paid and threatened to call the police.

'Open your legs,' Ntando said poised with cotton swab and pen barrel. She stuck two fingers inside Rachel and felt around for the baby. I hated having fingers stuck in me, it reminded me of going to the gynaecologist, except they used gloves.

'Ah, here it is,' she said, replacing her fingers with the pen barrel.

'It's running away!' she said as she pushed the barrel around in Rachel, who seemed quite relaxed.

'Aren't you feeling any pain?' I asked.

'No,' Rachel replied calmly, 'I can't feel anything.'

Suddenly Ntando pulled her fingers out of Rachel.

'What?' we both asked in alarm.

'It kicked me,' she said in disbelief.

'Eh, she's got a hard head,' Rachel said with a chuckle.

'Yes,' I added, 'like her mother.'

'Of course, what do you expect?' Rachel said proudly. Ntando smiled and pushed the barrel back into Rachel.

After a few moments of poking around inside Rachel, Ntando got a hold of what she was looking for and began puncturing it with the barrel. Each time she pushed in to stab, she bit her lower lip and squinted her eyes. I felt weak all over. My hands shook and my legs felt weak. I knelt down at the end of the bed and began stroking Rachel's hair – it was thick and nappy and smelt of coconut.

'You should start bleeding within the next few hours,' Ntando said as she handed the cotton to Rachel. 'Use this in your panties for now, it might start soon. When you start bleeding go to the hospital and tell them you're having a miscarriage,' she instructed.

As we walked back to the lobby the hallway seemed a lot narrower than before. The lobby was crowded. It was after five and men were pouring into the lounge for an after-work drink. The American tourists were out of place in the confusion. The woman sat on the backpack in tears while the man argued with the receptionist.

The rays of the setting sun streamed in through the tall doors of the entrance, highlighting the silhouettes of smoke from burning cigarettes while dust particles sparkled and danced above as we wove our way through the crowd.

I purposefully forgot to hand in the key. The Indian man already had more than one key for the room, didn't he? And besides, he still owed me five dollars change for the room. I threw it in the trashcan once we were outside.

We said goodbye to Ntando, who had resumed her nervousness and quickly disappeared into the rush-hour crowds. The tired-looking woman was now standing, looking a bit more energetic, her clothes flapping in a gentle breeze, as the peak of her business hours began. The baby was asleep on her back, strapped on with an old faded towel. The two older children had come out of the alley and were begging for money from prostitutes and their customers. Rachel lit a cigarette and we silently walked across the street to the train station to meet my mother who was parked in front of the building waiting for us to arrive from Harare.

As we approached the car I noticed that she was engrossed in a newspaper. I tapped on the window. She looked up in surprise and wound it down.

'Our train came in early, Mummy, so we went across to the hotel to get a drink,' I said immediately. 'I hope you weren't waiting too long,' I quickly added.

'No, it's all right, I actually just got here,' she said as she turned back to her paper.

'We have to go in and get our bags, Mummy,' I said as I looked back at Rachel, who was standing on the kerb. 'It shouldn't take a minute.' I turned to walk into the station building with Rachel.

Rachel had the key to the locker where we had left the bags early that morning. As she fished for the key in her purse she looked up at me and smiled; she still hadn't said a word since we had said goodbye to Ntando.

'Sisa, you worry too much,' she said as she placed the key in the lock and fiddled with it.

'Rachel, are you high or something?' I asked, now quite annoyed by Rachel's cool attitude about everything.

She looked at me and laughed. 'You take life too seriously, my girl,' she said as her face became more serious. 'At the rate you're going you'll have ulcers by the time you're twenty-five.'

She pulled out both our backpacks and threw mine at me.

'Let's go,' she said.

'Okay, but stay at my house tonight.'

'Only if we rent a movie.'

'Deal.'

'Are we all set?' Mummy asked, interrupting my thoughts, and putting down her newspaper.

'Yes, Mummy,' I sighed, 'but can we stop by the video store on the way home?' I looked back at Rachel, whose smile released me from my own anxiety. I was glad that Rachel had agreed to stay the night at our house – if she did start bleeding, at least we could drive her to the hospital. Her family didn't own a car. Besides, her mother had been in a frail state since Rachel's father had died a few months ago.

◆

That night, while my family was engrossed in an old kung-fu movie, Rachel started having cramps. When I went to the kitchen to get her some aspirin she got up to go to the bathroom. When she didn't come back after a good twenty minutes, I went to see if she was okay.

She wasn't. The bathroom was steamy and the shower was running. A trail of blood went from the toilet to the shower door. Her clothes were piled in the sink, which overflowed with rose-coloured water. I walked over to the open toilet and gagged at the sight of blood clots that looked like small pieces of liver. I walked over to the shower door.

'Rachel,' I called above the din of running water. 'How are you feeling?'

'Sisa,' she said weakly. 'I think I should go to the hospital. There's too much blood, man.' She clicked her teeth in annoyance.

'Oh my God,' I whispered. I rushed out of the bathroom, leaving the door open.

I ran down the hall towards my room, my heart beating in my ears. I frantically rehearsed what I was going to tell Mummy. I grabbed a towel, some fresh clothes and a pack of sanitary napkins. Tearing back down the hall towards the bathroom, I bumped into my younger sister, Lindani, and knocked her down. She looked up at me in horror. I had left the bathroom door open, she must have seen the blood. I barked over my shoulder, 'Go and tell Mummy we have to take Rachel to the hospital.'

Her reply was muffled as I rushed into the bathroom.

Rachel still hadn't come out of the shower.

'Rachel!' I yelled, banging on the shower door. I continuously struck the door with my fist. It gave way and flew open.

Rachel was curled up on the floor holding her stomach, her eyes closed tight. The water drummed her naked body, leading a trail of blood to the drain. I quickly turned off the shower and stepped in to help her up. There was blood, so much blood: the clots, the dark meaty clots.

She was obviously weak, but managed to get to her feet slowly as I draped a towel around her. I then led her to the toilet where I instructed her to sit down, while I tore open the bag of sanitary napkins and fitted one into clean underwear, helping her on with it.

With the shower off I could hear the sounds of the television in the lounge. Symphonic Chinese music played while I wiped the blood off the floor and helped Rachel put on her clothes. The music stopped. I was finished. There was a knock at the door.

'Sisa?' It was Mummy. 'Honey, what's going on in there?'

I felt like I was in a movie; like nothing was real. I wanted everything to end. I wished none of this had ever happened. I wanted to be a child again. I had lied to my mother and I couldn't fight it, I would give in.

I opened the door to a concerned face.

'What's going on?' she asked in a more frantic voice.

'We have to go to the hospital,' I said in a choked sob. 'Rachel is bleeding, she's having a miscarriage.'

I was picking at my nails. I was talking to my mother.

I told her about Ntando while I picked the hard nasty skin off my cuticles.

I told her about the chicken money while I bit at my forefinger.

I told her about the fake trip as I bit the nail on my baby finger.

But I looked at her and cried as I told her about the abortion.

ANNA DAO

A Perfect Wife

The word had swept in without warning. It took everyone by surprise, creating and provoking curiosity, torment, consternation, confusion, excitation and commotion everywhere. In the beginning it was confined to hushed whispers late at night over pillows, intended only for the ears of one's loving mate, and given with the firm recommendation to keep it under wraps.

Without anybody knowing how, the word had flown out and was found down on the market road where it was exchanged in veiled terms only for a vigorous promise never to let it out. Then it arrived and wandered under the shade of mango trees, to the edge of the well where the conclusion came after a firm assurance that it would never be peddled. It traipsed over family thresholds, and made its way into kitchens. Always in the end were the sworn intentions never to allow the slightest peep or leak. Tired at last, it was seen crawling under the palaver tree where it was whispered sombrely, and then it died at the sight of unidentified shadows.

Like spring rain, it had crossed the entire country. It was meted out prudently, parsimoniously, and always with the same never-ending imploration-exhortation: 'Above all, keep it to yourself. Never let it out.' Yet, it had spread like smoke, undermining and disturbing the life of the people in town, in the whole community. And now, after months of tension, deliberations, presumptions, suppositions and speculations the word was finally going to lose its illegitimacy, it would be publicly proclaimed and officially become the latest news.

With loud bugles of fanfare and tam-tam the occupying force[1] announced to the gathered crowd that in countries far beyond the salty waters, talk of powder and fire had just begun. And in order to defend his threatened territory, the good people of the occupied land would have to give up the courageous young men who were helping them work the land.

War! The word had now become official. From now on, war was a reality. Fear hung like a big rain cloud in the sky, ready to burst wide open. It slammed down upon their faces. A unified silent prayer rose and spilled over everyone's lips as a rumbling groan: 'War! *Soubahanalai!* God save us! Protect us!' The elders knew, the women understood, and the youth would soon find out.

◆

Sira was twelve years old. Married for only two months, she could not imagine the upheaval that this declaration would bring in her life. Chosen by Astou Koue, Idrissa Keita's first wife, Sira had been married to him in an attempt to bring what fifteen years of happy marriage had not brought: children.

A year earlier, Astou had sent for the *griot*[2] Sekouba Kouyate. She asked him to scout among the honourable neighbouring families and find a young girl who, though no longer a child, had not quite reached puberty, to become her co-spouse and share her space in Idrissa's bed. To carry out the difficult task entrusted to him, namely to find a young lady who would

[1] Colonizing French forces. At the time of World War I, a good number of West African countries were occupied by France. This included Mali, then known as the 'French Sudan'. In Mali the military penetration, or forced colonization, began around 1890 and ended on September 22, 1960 as the last French soldiers left and Mali gained independence.

[2] Community spokesperson with spiritual authority.

not only be the perfect wife for Idrissa, but would also know how to set aside Astou's 'due share of water'.[3]

Sekouba Kouyate decided to follow secretly and spy on all the girls of an age to be married. In the ensuing days, the *griot* would 'accidentally' run into them early in the morning on the paths to the market when they went to buy condiments, or by the rivers where they washed the family linen. By ten o'clock he would head into their homes to quench his thirst, share a cola nut and discuss the latest gossip with one of the elders of the house, while furtively observing every gesture and movement of the girl helping with household chores.

Thus, one by one, he eliminated the lazy girls, the girls who walked with their faces to the ground, those with elongated necks,[4] those with uncontrollable bursts of laughter,[5] those with irascible fathers or quarrelsome mothers.

One by one, the *griot* narrowed down the potential candidates, and soon held a small list of girls, among whom was Sira. Sekouba Kouyate liked her not only because she was sweet, docile and reserved, but also because her father, Oumar Keita, was a well-known and respected man in the community. Her mother, Mariam Coulibaly, everybody agreed, was a kind, affable and helpful woman, whose tongue was like a needle used to patch conflicts between members of her family as well as problems with neighbours. There was also the rather important fact that Sira had a wide mouth.[6]

Furthermore, the two families knew and respected each other, as they were both descended from the Keita ancestry

[3] The 'due share of water' of someone means the respect that is due to that person.

[4] According to superstition, a woman who walks with her face to the ground or has an elongated neck is looking or stretching her neck towards her husband or future fiancé's grave.

[5] People who laugh loudly or uncontrollably are generally considered as lacking discretion and self-control.

[6] A large or wide mouth is a sign of good luck.

with an illustrious warrior ancestor in common, Soundiata. Therefore, nothing stood in the way of the union between their households.

Sekouba Kouyate reported his research and selection to Astou, who in turn repeated the *griot*'s words to her husband, Idrissa. He approved and consented to ask for Sira in marriage.

And that is how, one evening after having said his *Safo* prayer, Sekouba Kouyate made his entrance into the home of Sira's father. After the greetings and customary chatting, the patriarch Oumar Keita asked him to explain the reason for his visit. Sekouba Kouyate revealed that he was the messenger sent by Idrissa Keita, first born of the now deceased Abdoulayes Keita and Sali Traore, who had sent him to raise his voice and inquire if the lovely and coveted gem named Sira already had her 'neck promised'[7] or if he could request to become a candidate and bring cola nuts?

Oumar Keita smiled and replied that he was not the right person to be asked that question. The *griot* should refer to his young brother Fatogoma, the father of the child.[8] Then, he called one of his sons and ordered him to take the *griot* to his brother's doorstep.

Fatogoma invited the *griot* in, listened to him and then explained that because he was not Sira's only father, he needed time to think and also consult with the others about what answer to give to the present request.[9]

[7] To be engaged.

[8] In Malian tradition, the natural parents of children are consulted in private by other family members, but have no right to take an active or visible part in organizing their offspring's wedding ceremony. They neither accept nor share the cola nuts or dowry. The child's paternal uncles and maternal aunts are the ones considered as his or her parents, with all the parental rights and duties. They are the ones who organize the wedding. In Malian society a child doesn't belong to the one who brought him into the world but rather to the entire community.

[9] Before deciding to accept or refuse a suitor's offer of cola nuts, families customarily request a period of several days to discuss the offer among themselves,

One month later, a nervous Sekouba Kouyate entered Fatogoma's hut for the second time where, to his great relief, he was told that he could inform his master Idrissa to bring the cola nuts.[10]

Once they had been accepted, and the dowry[11] had been ascertained and presented, the marriage between Idrissa and Sira was celebrated in style.

◆

To the blaring brass band and the drums they (the subjects) had been told about the necessity of their participation, however coerced and forced it might be, in the sabre rattling which felt completely foreign to them. 'They' the people, who had practised hospitality and welcomed 'visitors' only to wind up intruded upon, disposed of, shunned and set aside, were being called out and forced to defend the now anxious and nervous colonizer. The colonizer, who was afraid of the same fate he had once inflicted, now demanded 'their' assistance to help drive away and keep out a new intruder who was threatening

---

natural parents along with the 'fathers' and 'mothers'. They find out if there are other suitors, whether further investigation may be required, and try to get more information about the suitor's family (origin, respectability, etc.). Even for a couple betrothed at birth, it is not until the girl has had her first menstrual period (between ten and thirteen years of age) that the marriage can take place and the girl can leave her family to take her place in her husband's household.

[10] This would be the first of three cola nuts, which the *griot* brings one by one on three separate occasions, and which constitute the three stages of the official proposal. Three very large cola nuts, so that each father can take a bite. The first cola nut announces the future fiancé's candidacy. In accepting it, the family of the bride indicates that there are no other suitors or that they prefer him to all the others. Presenting the second cola nut, the suitor emphasizes that he is serious in his desire to marry their daughter. By accepting it, the family grants him permission. The third cola nut will then serve to confirm the proposal, as well as the bride's family's consent. Only after the third cola nut has been accepted will the young lady be officially informed that she is now engaged.

[11] After accepting the third cola nut, the fathers gather the mothers to ask them about the type of dowry, the customs and traditions to be respected.

to invade and take away his homeland, his history, and his lady love. To make them accept what was being offered, to simply consent to go out and get killed far away from their land, the 'ungrateful visitor' sent some of their own.

The good people were visited by their *griots*, their fathers, their chiefs, their elders, their wise men and their men of God.

The conqueror had ordered the *griots* to remind the people of their glorious past, so that once flattered, incited, and galvanized, they would only think and dream of fighting. The wise men and the men of God were ordered to reassure them and persuade them that their daily prayers, along with their families' sacrifices, would suffice to guarantee their safe return home.

The elders and fathers were herded together to hear talk of bonuses and the meagre benefits to be granted to their families, and of the honour and prestige awaiting those whose sons would go off to fight for such a noble cause.

Answering the calls of the conqueror (temporary master of their lands), and of their *griots*, fathers, chiefs, elders, wise men and men of God, the young brave men answered 'present' and then departed.

They departed with their ears still ringing with the *griot*'s chants and speeches about the exploits of their ancestors: heroic deeds that forbade all fear, desertion or mutilation.[12] They departed full of pride and happy to serve, even if it meant aiding some unknown land which, they had suddenly been informed, was also part of their home.

They departed because they were good sons who didn't know how to disobey their fathers.

[12] During mobilization, there were some regions where families did not want to give up their sons. Prior to the recruitment, the young men were given potions to drink that either made their sexual organs swell up, or made them appear seriously ill when they went for their medical exam. Those people would be disqualified for military service.

They departed because all their life, they had been taught to respect, and never contradict their elders, their chiefs, and their wise men. Those who did not volunteer were kidnapped and conscripted. Sometimes in broad daylight on the roadside, sometimes in their villages, or sometimes simply sitting at home and accused of vagrancy, they ended up, in spite of themselves, as soldiers. Whether they volunteered, were conscripts, or were simply rounded up in due course, they all appeared before a group of men[13] responsible for testing them and determining the ones worth mobilizing. The test weeded out the weaklings, the sickly, the scrawny and the puny. Some of them, indignant at having been refused on such slim grounds, protested and even swore to commit suicide if they were not enrolled.

Idrissa Keita enlisted voluntarily and, after having passed all the imposed tests, was placed in the group of privileged men who were going to wage war to protect and defend those who had made them captives in their own land.

When the news came about Idrissa's imminent departure to strange shores across the sea, his wives, sisters and brothers all got busy praying for God's mercy, to ensure his safe return among them. They consulted the stars again and again, and they asked cowry readers and geomancers to find out which offering or sacrifice would bend the will of the invisible forces that gave him protection.

Idrissa unflinchingly drank the sometimes sweet, sometimes bitter, potions his sisters brought, gulping down their strong-smelling and colourful concoctions without question. He patiently daubed his skin with all of the lotions his brothers gave him and, without coughing, he burned and sprinkled himself with the many powders and roots his two lovely wives placed before him. His body was adorned with the talismans

[13] The recruitment commission was usually composed of a major, an officer and a doctor.

that each had obtained for him. Great platters of food were prepared and given to the less fortunate. In his neighbourhood mosque, special prayers were said for him and for all those like him who were being 'confiscated' to be sent away.

A few days before his departure, Idrissa called his brothers Lamine and Jabril to his bedchamber for one last talk that went on into the small hours of the morning. That night, he assigned each of them the roles they would have to take on in his place. Lamine, the brother closest to his age, became the acting head of the family; the one to make all the decisions and ensure that the family needs were met. Jabril, the youngest, could read and write a little and his duty was to pick up Idrissa's monthly pay which he would then turn over to Lamine, who would give half to be split between Astou and Sira, and keep the other half for household expenses.

Afterwards, Idrissa went to say goodbye to his five sisters. Then, he sat down before his wives, asked them to 'give him the road',[14] and made them promise to look out for and take care of one another. With tears in their eyes Astou and Sira agreed to everything he said. Finally, he went to the homes of those who had seen him come into the world. And there, he bade his mothers and sisters farewell, then knelt before his fathers to receive their blessing. While bowing before each elder, a choked-up Idrissa felt their rough hands tremble as they laid them upon his head. Their voices quavered with emotion as they recited the *baraka*[15] benediction and safe return wishes while something deep inside them, like a

[14] A traveller must always symbolically ask his family and the people close to him for permission to leave. The request is followed by mutual forgiveness for all wrongdoings. As no man knows what lies ahead, nor who among his loved ones will still be present when he comes back, he must get his life in order before going out to travel. This tradition is still very much respected today.

[15] Good luck.

scratched record, kept on repeating that they would never be gathered together again.

The dreaded hour came. Festivities were held so that the banging tam-tam, accompanied by the singing and dancing, would cover up all the sighing and heaving footsteps of the budding warriors, muffle the mournful chants of the women, drown out the crying of abandoned children, and provide a distraction from the raspy sobbing of elders, who would crush the stubborn drops of water that refused to leave their eye-corners by nimbly taking up the end of their sleeves from time to time.

The beat of the tam-tam followed the soldiers to the camp where they were taught some of the basics of military life. More celebrations took place along their route to the station where a train took them to their next destination – a port. There, they were crammed into a ship, a thousand or two at a time, for their passage across the salty waters. The voyage ended ten days later when Idrissa and his companions landed on the shores of the land they were now to defend.

When they arrived, the sons of the desert were issued uniforms identical to those worn by their hosts. Instead of helmets, though, each man received a lovely brightly-coloured fez which was supposed to remind him of his home. They were also given huge, oversized shoes that had been made especially for them, but their poor little feet slid around in them.

Since they had been warned that long daily walks caused the arriving troops' feet to swell, after a great deal of thinking and consideration, the fine shoemakers had concluded that if running could widen the foot, it most certainly had to lengthen it too. Blinded by the irrefutable logic and good sense of their deduction, the good men set to work and manufactured immense cloddish combat boots which paddled the soldiers' slim feet. All decked out, the children of the tropics were sent to the front where they endured the deadly combination of the cold weather and cannonball fire.

Even with the head of the family gone, life resumed its rhythm of births and deaths, sowing, harvesting, and cooking days.[16] In addition, the arrival of the monthly allocation came, the information-propaganda selected and spread by the occupying force, the rumours that could not be contained and, of course, letters from Idrissa.

Like most of his illiterate comrades, Idrissa took his correspondence to one of the young educated soldiers who, during his free time, became their letter-writers. Each letter began the same way: 'I am writing to you to give you my news. I'm fine and hope that this letter will find you fine too. Nothing wrong here.' And then a blank – a total blank. What else was there to say? Where could he start? What words could he possibly find to describe the daily horror that their lives had become? Shipped in by the thousand from all parts of the African continent, they were the pawns, the disposable and dispensable, used as sacrifices in order to avoid shedding the blood of the 'better men' – those other humans whose useful, precious existences deserved to be spared, preserved and saved.

Condemned to endless hours of toil in the trenches, they spent days in icy rainwater with swollen and chafed feet confined to boots designed just for them. They did their best to face and resist the devastating, exterminating assaults of the enemy who wiped out a good number of them each day. To escape flying bullets, they piled up dead bodies as barriers and hid behind them. There were so many bullet-ridden, mangled bodies, as well as the bodies of those who had let themselves go and had been eaten by illness: the last remains of poor souls

---

[16] In polygamous families, cooking days are equally divided among the wives. Usually, each wife cooks for two consecutive days, corresponding to the two days she shares her husband's bed.

whom they hadn't had time to bury and whose outrages would come back later to haunt them and prevent them from sleeping.

To keep their sanity they would gather and huddle together whenever they could. To keep from shivering, they would sit tightly bunched, pressed against each other for hours, warming their bodies and their hearts with talk of their countries, their families and of all the things they would do if they ever made it back home.

Jabril would read to the family the few lines that usually made up Idrissa's letters. Reassured, Astou and Sira spent night after night spinning cotton and talking about him. Astou talked endlessly, and Sira listened tirelessly, drinking up everything she was told. Distrustful at first, not knowing what to tell and what to keep to herself, Astou had grown fond of Sira, who was a cheerful, sweet girl who never got tired of keeping Astou company even when she really didn't want to: Sira, the girl recommended by the *griot*, whom she had pushed Idrissa to marry. Astou was certain that Sira, her co-spouse, would always give her her due share of water even when she would have Idrissa's children. Little by little, Astou opened up to her attentive rival Sira who, without realizing it, was learning to better know and love the man who was also her husband.

While unveiling her past and narrating to Sira, Astou went back in time and relived how she had become Idrissa's wife. Idrissa had been part of the household, a son of the house, a childhood friend of her older brothers who had 'put on pants'[17] at the same time they did. Just like them, she had known him all of her life. He had always been there, quick to support her and to smile at her. Every time their paths crossed as she

[17] Circumcision ceremony. It used to be that boys were circumcised around the age of fifteen. All youths of the same age group, born the same year, were circumcised together on the same day. The boys' families joined efforts a year before to prepare the event. It is a big celebration for a boy's entry into manhood.

walked past the group of boys, her brothers and the others would wink at each other and burst into laughter. They would yell out: 'Hey guys, outta the way! Here comes Idrissa's wife.' They'd crack up, holding their sides, while an embarrassed and silent Idrissa kicked the dust or some imaginary stone. A flustered Astou would look down, hasten her steps and rush to disappear.

As time went by and Astou grew up, her figure changed and took on new curves. When she reached the age to be requested, Idrissa, ready and impatient to get married, went to see his favourite father. He begged him to hasten the *griot* with cola nuts before anyone else beat him to it and stole away his beloved for ever. Amused, the father of the impetuous lover nevertheless took the time to consult other family members before sending his emissary to ask Astou's parents for the release of their daughter for his son Idrissa. Permission was granted, and the union was sealed with joy.

The two women talked about war. Sira was afraid she would never again see the man she had discovered and come to love through her co-spouse's words. Although she was worried and shared the same anxiety, most of all, Astou was jealous that her rival could speak so freely about her feelings. 'The nerve!' she thought. 'How dare she be as apprehensive as I am about my Idrissa?'

Days, months and years passed, punctuated by the return of a few insane and mutilated men, the mournful wails of parents who had their sons reported 'dead' or 'missing in action', and the growing love of two women for the absent Idrissa.

And then suddenly, from out of nowhere, the rumour landed, headed inland and spread like wildfire. Confirmed, the rumour became truth: the war was over. The men were coming home. Some in one piece, but many only half human with ravaged faces and atrophied bodies. Others, beaten by the multiple forces quarrelling within them, had become disturbed and deranged.[18] They were all going to be reunited and once the euphoria of the homecoming was over, many would find it hard to readapt and fit in among those who had learned to get by and managed without them.

One morning, Astou and Sira cleaned and incensed Idrissa's bedchamber together. They laughed and sang as they cooked, ignoring the exchange of their brothers-in-law's knowing smiles, and their sisters-in-law's looks of innuendo. They overlooked the whispering of their uncles and aunts, and the grins on the faces of the elders and neighbours, all of whom had come for the long-awaited arrival of Idrissa. Lamine, Jabril and a few close friends had already gone to the train station to greet him.

As the hours passed by, the joyfulness and excitement were replaced by anxiety, doubt, aggravation, and irritation. A premonition that something was wrong germinated, but was immediately suppressed by excuses invented by exasperated minds, that stubbornly wanted to believe that nothing could have happened.

Then out of nowhere he came, appearing before them – the Imam entered the yard followed by a few wise men. Their grave faces brought shattering silence. They were quickly seated and given water to drink so that they could say the words they had come to deliver. Sira sat down. Astou, with shaky legs and buzzing head, stood immobile. The man of God drank, gave thanks, cleared his throat and, looking at the

[18] In Malian tradition, there is a contrast between the 'Person' which is the human body and 'the persons of the Person', also called 'doubles' or 'forces', which are the psyche, the mind. The human body is the temple and the site where all these often contradictory forces, in perpetual conflict, come together. Illnesses are the result of too much agitation of the forces, and a loss of control of the body who can no longer contain them. When disturbances cannot be exteriorized, they get turned into internal problems (e.g. depression, mental illness, madness, etc.).

ground declared: 'What God gives, He takes back when and where He wants.'

Astou's mind clouded, emptied. She slid. Hands grabbed her and sat her down on the mat next to Sira. Men grasped their prayer beads. A murmured '*A ka dogo Allah ye*'[19] could be heard, while Idrissa's sisters and the neighbourhood ladies let out their first screams of disbelief, despair and devastation.

Dead! Gone! Idrissa, without their knowing it, had eaten his share of salt, drunk his share of water. And while they were preparing for his welcome-home festivity, he had gone to rest in peace. Numb, Sira listened, and understood. Slowly, tears streamed down her face. Like a wounded animal, Astou shrieked, heaved and choked. Their pain was fanned and kindled each time they heard the keening of the sisters-in-law and the other women.

Having announced the news, the Imam and his followers got up and left. Astou and Sira were taken to Idrissa's bedchamber, a room they had so lovingly arranged a few hours earlier and in which they were now going to be isolated for the next 132 days.[20] They were placed side by side on two mats laid on the ground. Then, according to tradition, their sisters-in-law sang their praises while taking out their braids.[21] After the ritual, Astou and Sira were bathed and given their mourning clothes.[22]

[19] 'Everything that happens is tiny compared to God.' The formula is used to explain our helplessness when confronted with fate.

[20] 132 days or four months and ten days. For that whole period, the widows are not allowed to leave their home. This time of isolation also makes it possible to determine if any of the widows were pregnant at the time of the husband's death.

[21] Upon the death of the husband, his sisters untangle the widows' hair and while doing so, they console the wives, reminding them of all their good deeds. They vow to take over from their deceased brother and promise to assist and help them as he would have done. Of course this only happens if there is a good relationship between the wives and their husband's family.

[22] A widow's mourning garb is made of a loincloth, a 'mini boubou', which is a sort of long halter top, and a large scarf that completely covers the head. The clothes are in cotton dyed in a certain shade of blue that is only used for widowhood.

Idrissa's companions came to express their condolences. Some of them were speechless; stricken to the soul. Their whole being refused to grasp and accept what had happened. But there were the others who tried to articulate and let out the words of what had happened, knowing how his family hungered for details and thirsted for knowledge. They developed and described, wove words interspersed with long silences, for they knew neither when nor how to stop. It is through their words and explanations, jealously collected and preserved, that the family came to understand the irony of Idrissa's tragic end.

The war was over. Idrissa had not been hurt. Along with many wounded infantrymen, he had embarked on a boat for a two-week voyage that brought them closer to home. Idrissa was anxious to be back; anxious to see Astou and Sira. He longed to see Astou, to whom he would tell his ordeal, and recount his moments of fright. Astou, against whom he would snuggle up to ward off and cast out his harassing, hounding demons. Astou, who would find ways to appease his soul and liberate him from his invisible persecutors.

And then there was Sira, who would revive and invigorate him with her youth, allow him finally to experience the joy of fatherhood.

Idrissa had made it to the tropical shores and the nearby station. A train was to take him back home two days later. On the eve of their return to their birthplace, Idrissa and his comrades went out one last time to admire the immensity of the salty waters and to fill their lungs with its special air. With eyes closed, and trembling with gratitude, they thanked the heavens and the hidden forces that had watched over them. Then, like children, they tossed off their army boots and dug their toes into the wet sand. The sun was setting when they decided that they'd had enough and that it was time to head back.

They had walked a short way away from the water when a shrill call ripped through the silence causing their feet to turn around. They ran back, their fiery eyes aglow as they scrutinized and searched the stretch of ocean. Then one of them hollered out as he pointed his finger towards the horizon where something was moving. The thing appeared, rocked, bobbed up and down, disappeared, then reappeared again. Forgetting that he didn't know how to swim, Idrissa rushed towards the struggling, slapping hand that was blindly, frantically searching for something solid to grab. He reached the desperate man, who seized him and curled his arms round him. The man hugged Idrissa tighter and tighter against him until Idrissa choked. Then, arms flailing, they started swirling and rolling over. They popped up, jostled by the flow of water, and then sank. Over and over, they rose to the surface, and were carried further and further away by the furious sea that held them as prisoners. When the waters finally calmed down, gentle waves separated the two men, and then brought Idrissa back to the shore, abandoning their hold and depositing his drowned, lifeless body at the feet of his petrified friends.

Later that day, unknown hands washed and anointed him, then enshrouded him in seven metres of white percale,[23] the gift of some compassionate soul. Thus prepared, Idrissa was carried by his friends to the cemetery where he was laid to rest.

Those who had gone to the train station to pick him up were stopped on their way and taken to the mayor who, having been informed, had the bitter task of breaking the news.

The Imam, his followers and the repatriated soldiers came back in the afternoon to pray with the community for the

[23] This is the only clothing allowed for the burial of a Muslim.

eternal rest of the deceased. The man of God asked Idrissa's wives and all those who had known or had come close to him, to forgive the man who had left them.

> Furious, they forgave.
> Helpless, they forgave.
> Filled with grief, they forgave.
> Angry and bitter, they forgave.
> Days became weeks and weeks became months.

During that time, the two women lived together, cut off from the rest of the world. Their friendship blossomed as never before, and their dependency on each other grew. They rolled in pity, whined and got mad. They shared the mourning, the food, the questions, the resentment, the emptiness and the loneliness. When Astou sobbed, Sira consoled and calmed her. She pulled her close to her, held her and rocked her until Astou fell asleep, finally worn out.

For four months and ten days – with the streams of visitors coming and going, with the old times to recall, the fits of laughter together with the tears and regrets it provoked – Sira comforted and cared for Astou. She watched over her co-spouse, forcing her to eat, to remember and to talk. And little by little, Astou relived and came to tell Sira of the last part of her life with Idrissa. The years of joy and longing when they had tried everything to conceive and have a baby. She told of the diets, the prayers, and the alms-giving – and always nothing. Astou's uterus remained barren. Finally she gave up hope of bearing Idrissa's child and learned to tolerate the idea of sharing him. Idrissa was reluctant at first. Even after she had accepted the idea of a co-spouse to give Idrissa children, he still wanted to wait and try. Finally, on her insistence, he agreed to take on a second wife on the condition that she, Astou, would choose the one who would become his bride. Feeling awkward and not knowing how to go about it, Astou in turn had called upon Sekouba Kouyate to help her out.

After the four months and ten days, Astou and Sira left their mourning clothes for the new outfits which were gifts from Idrissa's family. They went to visit all the family members and close friends who had come to assist and comfort them during the mourning period.[24] Then, Astou and Sira each went to their father's home 'to bury the last tears for the death'.[25]

When they came back, the family held a meeting to decide on their future. Lamine, Jabril and Idrissa's five sisters wanted them to stay. They were part of the family. Lamine had two wives, but offered to take Astou as the third. Jabril had only one wife and wanted to marry Sira. Astou wished to remain, but without remarrying, and Sira consented to start a new life with Jabril.

Nine years later, and after five false starts where 'the babies had fallen',[26] a delighted Astou was watching over an exhausted, confined Sira, drained by seven months of imposed rest and the stranger that continually moved and wiggled inside her. Astou joked that she was pretty sure that the expected happy event would be a girl.

'If that were the case,' Sira replied, 'everybody would know who to name the baby after.'

Astou feigned offence and asked what Sira meant. Was she referring to her?

Sira quickly replied, 'No, no,' and then muttered under her breath, 'who else in this house is almost as difficult?'

'I heard that,' yelled out Astou. Then they laughed.

Astou didn't wait. She went away a few days later, tiptoeing

[24] After the mourning period, the widows must visit and thank family members and close friends who were there for them.
[25] To officially end the mourning period, the widows have to leave the place of mourning for a few days and then come back.
[26] This expression means miscarriage.

out so as not to disturb anyone. She passed away seated on her rug at the end of the morning prayer, after having been reassured by the one calling her that Sira no longer really needed her. She was told that Sira would know how to manage, and how to go on without her from that point on. Astou smiled, let out a relieved sigh, and then went up to join the one who had come for her: Idrissa.

Two months and three days later, a girl was born. A fulfilled Sira smiled.

To keep her promise and honour their friendship, as well as to perpetuate her memory and give the newborn an identity, Sira and her kin decided that the child could only have one name. Thus, each time one of them would call her, all would remember the one who had left them. Later, Sira would tell baby Astou about her other mother, who had loved her and watched over her, but couldn't stay long enough to wait for her arrival. She would lovingly describe Astou in detail, so the child would adopt Astou's qualities and make them her own.

On the seventh day after her birth, old Sekouba Kouyate took the newborn in his arms and with tears in his voice whispered three times in her right ear and then three times in her left ear: 'Your name is Astou. Your name is Astou. Your name is Astou.'

MILLY JAFTA

The Home-Coming

The bus came to a standstill and all the passengers spilled out as soon as they could. It was Friday, end of the week, end of the month, end of the year, and the trip from Windhoek to the north was hot and unending. Unlike previous times, I remained in my seat until the bus was empty. Then I gathered my belongings and moved to the door. Through the window I could see Maria scrambling to claim my two suitcases.

The heat of the late afternoon sun hit me as I alighted from the bus. The warmth outside was different from the human heat that I felt inside the bus. Now the smell of sweat and over-spiced fast food seemed like a distant memory. The welcome smell of meat over-exposed to the sun filled my nostrils. I could even hear the buzzing of the metallic-green coloured flies as they circled and landed on the meat hanging from the tree branches and the makeshift stalls. Circled and landed, circled and landed . . . Hawkers and buyers were busy closing the last deals of the day. The air was filled with expectancy.

Maria bent down and kissed me on the lips – a dry and unemotive gesture. She smiled, picked up the larger of the two suitcases and placed it on her head. Then she started walking ahead of me. I picked up the other case, placed it on my head and put both my hands in the small of my back to steady myself. Then I followed her. I looked at Maria's straight back, the proud way she held her head and the determination with which she walked. How beautiful is the unbroken human spirit. I tried desperately to think of something to say, but could not find the words. Thoughts were spinning in my head,

178

but my mouth remained closed and empty. So we continued in silence, this stranger – my daughter – and I.

So this was it. My home-coming. What did I expect? The village to come out in celebration of a long-lost daughter who had come home? How long had it been? Forty years? It must have been about forty years. How I have lost track of the time. How could I be expected to keep track of the time, when I could only measure it against myself in a foreign land? When I planted seeds but never had the chance to see them grow, bore children but never watched them grow . . . when I had to make myself understood in a foreign tongue . . . had to learn how an electric kettle works, how and when to put the stove off, that doors are not opened to strangers, and that you do not greet everyone you meet with a handshake.

I tried not to look at the long dusty road ahead of us. In any case there was nothing in particular to look at. Everything seemed barren and empty. No trees, no grass, just the sprawling brown and orange ground all around us. The last rays of the sun seemed to lighten it to a golden glow. I am sure this would make a beautiful colour picture: the two of us walking behind each other in the narrow path with my luggage on our heads, silhouetted against the setting sun. One December I saw a large picture like that, only it was of giraffe. I remember standing there, looking at it and for a moment longing to smell the fields after the rain. But I was in Swakopmund with my *Miesies*[1] and her family as she needed the rest. It was holiday time, family time, but I was without my own family, just as I was for the rest of the year and for most of my adult life.

Now all that has changed. I am on my way home. I am walking the same path as I walked many years ago. Only then I was seventeen and my eyes looked forward. A young girl has

[1] Mistress of a household.

left and now – after forty years, three children and a couple of visits to the village – an old woman is on her way back home. An old woman who has her eyes fixed to the ground.

My daughter, the stranger, stopped suddenly. Turned around and looked inquiringly at me. I realized that she must have been waiting for an answer or a reaction of some sort. I was so lost in my thoughts that I had no idea what she was waiting for. But then, I never had any idea what my children's actual needs were. In her calm voice she repeated the question, asking whether she was walking too fast for me. Oh dear God, what kindness. Someone was actually asking me whether I could keep up. Not telling me to walk faster, to have no males in my room, to get up earlier, to pay more attention, to wash the dog . . . I was overcome. Tears filled my eyes. My throat tightened, but my spirit soared. The stranger, my daughter, took the case from her head and put it on the ground next to her. Then she helped me to take my case down from my head and placed it next to hers.

'Let us rest for a while,' she said gently. After we sat down on the cases next to each other she said: 'It is so good to have you home.'

We sat there in complete silence, with only the sound of some crickets filling the air. I never felt more content, more at peace. I looked at the stranger and saw my daughter. Then I knew I had come home. I did matter. I was together with the fruit of my womb. I had grown fruit. I looked down at my wasted, abused body and thought of the earth from which such beautiful flowers burst forth.

'We must go now. Everybody is waiting for you,' Maria said, standing up. 'You walk in front. You set the pace, I will follow you.'

I walked ahead of Maria in the narrow path, my back straight and my eyes looking forward. I was in a hurry to reach home.

Notes on Contributors

Leila Aboulela, born in Cairo in 1964, is half Egyptian, half Sudanese. She grew up in Khartoum and graduated from the University of Khartoum in 1985, later studying statistics at the London School of Economics. She now lives in Aberdeen with her husband and three children. She has written stories for BBC Radio and for a number of Scottish anthologies. Her first novel, *The Translator*, is to be published in 1999.

Ama Ata Aidoo was born in central Ghana in 1942 and obtained a BA in English at the University of Ghana in 1964. She studied creative writing at Stanford University, California, and has worked as a lecturer at a number of universities and academic and research institutions in Ghana, other parts of Africa and the United States. During the 1980s she served as Secretary for Education in the Ghanaian government. Her publications include *The Dilemma of a Ghost* (1965), *No Sweetness Here* (1969), *Anowa* (1970), *Our Sister Killjoy* (1973), *Someone Speaking to Sometime* (1985), *The Eagle and the Chickens and Other Stories* (1986) and *Changes* (1991). She now divides her time between Ghana and the United States.

Lindsey Collen was born in the Transkei in South Africa and has lived in Mauritius with her husband, Ram Seegobin, since 1974. She has written five novels: *There is a Tide* (1991), *The Rape of Sita* (1994), *Misyon Garson* (1996), *Getting Rid of It* (1997) and *Mutiny*. *The Rape of Sita* was awarded the Commonwealth Writers Prize for best African book in 1994. Her work, often controversial, has been translated into German, Dutch, French and Danish.

Anna Dao was born in Paris and spent her childhood in a number of countries with her father, a diplomat, and her grandmother. She completed her education in Canada and for several years afterwards lived in Mali, working for various United Nations agencies. During the same period she produced and hosted a public-affairs talk show for Radio Kledu and wrote a column for the weekly newspaper *Le Républicain*. She left Mali for the United States at the end of 1993 and is now living and writing in New York.

Milly Jafta, who originally trained as a social worker, works as a researcher in Windhoek, Namibia. Coming from a family of orators and storytellers, she started writing at school and continues to this day for the 'sheer joy of creating'. She is the co-writer of the filmscript *The Homecoming*, part of the Africa Dreaming Project. Also an amateur actress, she describes her great passion in life as 'making the unsung heroines of the world more visible'.

Farida Karodia was born and raised in South Africa and went into exile in Canada in 1969. Her writing career began with radio dramas for the CBC and she has also written for film and television. Her publications include *Daughters of the Twilight* (1986), *Coming Home and Other Stories* (1988), *A Shattering of Silence* (1991) and *Against an African Sky* (1994). Her stories have also appeared in several anthologies. She divides her time between Canada and South Africa.

Norma Kitson is South African and has been a member of the ANC for over forty years. During her husband's imprisonment as a member of the High Command of Umkhonto we Sizwe, she and her two children lived in exile in London, where they founded the City of London Anti-Apartheid Group. Her auto-biography, *Where Sixpence Lives*, was published in 1986 to great acclaim. Articles, short stories and book reviews by Norma Kitson have appeared in numerous international magazines and journals, and she is the editor of two volumes of the *Zimbabwe Women Writers Anthology* and of *Teardrops: The Poems of Fanuel Jongwe*. She has run a number of creative-writing workshops and is the author of *Creative Writing: A Handbook* (1997). She also founded Red Lion Setters, the first women's typesetting collective.

Sindiwe Magona was born in South Africa and grew up on the Cape Town Flats. A teacher and social worker, she raised her three children, now adults, by herself. She obtained an education by correspondence and later won a scholarship to Columbia University, New York, where she graduated with an MS from the School of Social Work. Since 1984 she has worked for the Department of Public Information at the United Nations, New York. She is the author of two volumes of autobiography, *To My Children's Children* and *Forced to Grow*, as well as two collections of short stories, *Living, Loving, and Lying Awake at Night* and *Push-Push and Other Stories*. Her first novel, *Mother to Mother*, is based on the killing of American Fulbright scholar Amy Biehl in South Africa in 1993.

Lília Momplé was born on the island of Moçambique, off the northern coast of Mozambique, in 1935 and obtained a BA in social work in Portugal. She has represented her country at a number of international cultural assemblies, including the UNESCO General Assembly in Paris, participated in the Iowa International Writing Programme in 1997 and has lectured on Mozambican literature at universities in the United States and France. She has published two collections of short stories, *No*

One Killed Suhura (1988) and *The Green Eyes of the Cobra* (1997), a novel, *Neighbours* (1995), and a television drama, *Muhipiti – Alina* (1998). She is President of the Association of Mozambican Writers and a member of the board of the Southern African Writers' Council.

Chiedza Musengezi was born in 1954, grew up in Zimbabwe (formerly Rhodesia) and studied at the University of Zimbabwe. She is a member of Zimbabwe Women Writers and several of her short stories and poems have appeared in ZWW anthologies. A participant in the Iowa International Writing Programme in 1993, she worked as a teacher before becoming an editor with a firm of publishers.

Melissa Tandiwe Myambo is from Zimbabwe and is studying comparative literature in New York. Her work has appeared in the *Journal of African Travel Writing* and 'Deciduous Gazettes' is part of a forthcoming collection entitled *Jacaranda Journals*.

Gugu Ndlovu was born in Zambia in 1976 to a Canadian mother and a Zimbabwean father. The family moved to Zimbabwe after Independence in 1980. Gugu Ndlovu travelled to the United States in 1994 to attend Howard University, Washington DC, and now lives and writes in New York. She is married and has one son.

Ifeoma Okoye teaches English at Nnamdi Azikiwe University, Akwa, Nigeria. Her prize-winning novel *Behind the Clouds* (1983) was followed by two more novels: *Men Without Ears* (1985), which won the Best Fiction of the Year Award from the Association of Nigerian Authors and was translated into Russian, and *Chimere* (1992). She has also written children's books, two of which, *Village Boy* (1978) and *Only Bread for Eze* (1985), won literary prizes. Three of her children's books have been translated into Kiswahili. She lives with her children and her husband, a nationalist and writer, in Enugu.

Monde Sifuniso was born in 1944 and grew up in the Western Province of Zambia, formerly known as Barotseland. Her higher qualifications include a teaching certificate from the University College of Rhodesia and Nyasaland, a certificate in educational broadcasting from the Australian Broadcasting Corporation Training School and a diploma in advanced publishing studies from Oxford Brookes University. She is co-editor of and contributor to a volume of short stories, *The Heart of a Woman* (1997), and a book on Zambian women politicians, *Woman Power in Politics* (1998). Her research into the way people in the province of Western Zambia perceive their health was published as *Talk About Health* (1998). Monde Sifuniso retired as University of Zambia publisher in 1997. She is president of the Zambia Women Writers' Association and publicity secretary for the Non-Governmental Organisations Co-ordinating Committee in Zambia.

Véronique Tadjo grew up in Côte d'Ivoire and obtained a BA in English from the University of Abidjan, followed by a PhD in African-American literature and civilization from the Sorbonne, Paris. In 1983 she was awarded a Fulbright Research Scholarship to Howard University, Washington DC; she was subsequently a lecturer at the University of Abidjan, until 1993. Her volume of poetry, *Latérite* (published in 1984), won the literary prize of the Agence de Cooperation Culturelle et Technique in 1983. She is the author of three novels: *A Vol d'Oiseau* and *Le Royaume Aveugle* (both 1992) and *Champs de Bataille et d'Amour* (1999). She has also written and illustrated several books for young people. Having lived in Paris, Lagos, Mexico City and Nairobi, Véronique Tadjo is now based in London.

Acknowledgements

The publishers would like to thank the following copyright holders for permission to reproduce the short stories in this anthology:

Ama Ata Aidoo for 'The Girl who Can'; Melissa Tandiwe Myambo for 'Deciduous Gazettes'; Lindsey Collen for 'The Enigma'; Farida Karodia for 'The Red Velvet Dress'; Norma Kitson for 'Uncle Bunty'; Véronique Tadjo for 'The Betrayal'; Leila Aboulela for 'The Museum', which was first published in *Ahead of its Time* edited by Duncan McLean (Jonathan Cape, 1997); Ifeoma Okoye for 'The Power of a Plate of Rice'; Lília Momplé for 'Stress'; Sindiwe Magona for 'A State of Outrage'; Chiedza Musengezi for 'Crocodile Tales'; Monde Sifuniso for 'Night Thoughts'; Gugu Ndlovu for 'The Barrel of a Pen'; Anna Dao for 'A Perfect Wife', © Anna Dao 1999; Milly Jafta for 'The Home-Coming'. 'The Home-Coming' first appeared in *Coming on Strong*, published by New Namibia Books.